FAST TRACK TO READING

Accelerated Learning for EFL and ESOL Students
Course Book

Peter Viney

Garnet EDUCATION

Credits

Acknowledgements

Published by
Garnet Publishing Ltd.
8 Southern Court
South Street
Reading RG1 4QS, UK

ISBN: 978 1 85964 489 8

British Library Cataloguing-in-Publication Data
A catalogue record for this book is available from the British Library.

Production

Project manager:	Kate Brown
Pedagogical consultant:	Anna Phillips
Editorial team:	Kate Brown, Emily Clarke
Design:	Mike Hinks
Layout:	Dany Awad
Photography:	ClipArt; Corbis: Daniella Cesarei/Loop Images, Christie's Images, Andrew Fox, Tom Grill, George Hall, Moodboard, Jose Fuste Raga, Transtock and Whisson/Jordan; Hemera and Peter Viney

Every effort has been made to trace the copyright holders, and we apologize in advance for any unintentional omissions. We will be happy to insert the appropriate acknowledgements in any subsequent editions.

Printed and bound in Lebanon by International Press.

p59 *iPod logo*: Apple, the Apple logo, iPod, iTunes, and Mac are trademarks of Apple Inc., registered in the U.S. and other countries. Apple TV and iPhone are trademarks of Apple Inc. iPod is for legal or rightholder-authorized copying only. Don't steal music.
TDK logo: TDK is a registered trademark of TDK Corporation.

p61 *MP3 logo*: MPEG Layer-3 audio coding technology logo courtesy of Fraunhofer IIS and Thomson.

p75 *Royal Mail logo*: Cruciform (Standard) © and Trade Marks of Royal Mail Group Ltd. Reproduced by kind permission of Royal Mail Group Ltd. All rights reserved.

p95 *Google logo*: © Google Inc., 2009. Reprinted with Permission.
iTunes Logo: Apple, the Apple logo, iPod, iTunes, and Mac are trademarks of Apple Inc., registered in the U.S. and other countries. Apple TV and iPhone are trademarks of Apple Inc. iPod is for legal or rightholder-authorized copying only. Don't steal music.

p107 *BA concourse*: www.baa.com/photolibrary

We would like to thank Apple, Aston Villa Football Club, BAA Aviation Photo Library, Blackburn Rovers Football & Athletic PLC, Boeing Images, Bradford Bulls, Caterpillar, DVD Format/Logo Licensing Corporation, FIFA, Fraunhofer IIS, Honda, Google, National Geographic, Royal Mail, Sony Europe, TDK Corporation, Thomson, Toyota Motor Europe NV/SA, United States Postal Service, Aston Villa Football Club and The Wrigley Company for granting us permission to use their copyright material in this publication.

Contents

4

To the student

Are you unable to read in English using the Roman alphabet? If so, this reading programme is designed for you.

Reading in English is fundamental to learning the language and will help you access course books that can help you learn the language.

This reading programme will help you with the first step to learning English: learning to **read** in English.

Learning to read is a process that takes time, so don't do more than one unit a day. You will make progress by working through the whole programme, so do not try to remember everything at once.

Do you read too slowly in English using the Roman alphabet?

This programme will help you read more quickly. You will not only learn to read faster but will also learn to read difficult words.

You may find the first few units very easy. If so, go through them quickly.

Important points to note:

- This course will **not** teach you the English language. It will teach you how to **read** the Roman alphabet quickly and easily.

- You will **not** understand all the words. Don't worry about this. You are learning to put the sounds with the words. This will help you later, when you are learning the English language.

- Do **not** try to translate the words. This will make progress with the programme much too slow.

إلى التلميذ

○ إذا لم تكن قادراً على قراءة الإنجليزية بأبجديتها اللاتينية، فإن هذا البرنامج التعليمي المُعَد لتعلّم قراءتها مخصّص لك.

إنّ قراءة الإنجليزية مهارة أساسية لتعلّم اللغة، فإذا أجدتها سيكون بوسعك أن تستخدم كتب المقرّر التعليمي كي تتعلّم هذه اللغة.

إنّ هذا البرنامج المُعَد خصيصًا لتعليم القراءة سيساعدك في الخطوة الأولى لتعلّم الإنجليزية: قراءة الإنجليزية.

إنّ تعلّم القراءة عملية تستغرق الكثير من الوقت. لذلك يجب أن تكتفي بتعلّم درس واحد في اليوم. لا تحاول أن تتذكّر كل شيء دفعة واحدة، لأنك ستحرز التقدم كلما تقدمت في دراسة هذا المقرّر.

○ هل تقرأ الإنجليزية بأبجديتها اللاتينية بوتيرة بطيئة جدًا؟

إنّ هذا البرنامج سيساعدك على القراءة بوتيرة أسرع. ولن تتعلّم القراءة بوتيرة أسرع فحسب، بل ستتعلّم أيضًا قراءة الكلمات الصعبة.
قد تجد الوحدات القليلة الأولى سهلة جدًا. إذا كان الأمر كذلك، فلا تتوقف عندها طويلاً، بل أنجزها بسرعة لتنتقل إلى الوحدات الأصعب.

○ ملاحظات مهمّة

• هذا المقرّر التعليمي لن يعلّمك اللغة الإنجليزية. هذا المقرّر سيعلّمك كيف تقرأ الأبجدية اللاتينية بسرعة وسهولة.

• ستكتشف أنّك لا تفهم كل الكلمات في هذا المقرّر. لا تقلق لهذا الأمر، فأنت تتعلّم إعطاء الكلمة أصواتها. وهذا سيساعدك فيما بعد، أثناء تعلّم اللغة الإنجليزية.

• لا تحاول أن تترجم الكلمات. إنّ هذه الطريقة ستُبطئ كثيرًا عملية التقدم في هذا المقرّر التعليمي.

طلبائی کیلئے

کیا آپ - رومی حروف تحجی انگریزی میں پڑھنے کے قابل نہیں ہیں؟ اگر ایسا ہے تو یہ پڑھنے کا پروگرام آپ کیلئے مرتب کیا گیا ہے۔

انگریزی میں پڑھنا، زبان سیکھنے کی بنیاد ہے اور کورس کی کتابیں جو آپکو زبان سیکھنے میں مدد کر یں گی، تک رسائی حاصل کرنے میں آپکی مدد کر سکے۔

یہ پروگرام انگریزی سیکھنے کا پہلا قدم، انگریزی پڑھنے میں، آپکی مدد کرے گا۔

پڑھائی سیکھنے کا مکمل وقت طلب ہے، پس ایک دن میں ایک سبق سے زیادہ نہ کریں۔ آپ تمام پروگرام کے دوران ترقی کریں گے، اسلئے سب کچھ ایک ہی وقت میں یاد کرنے کی کوشش مت کریں۔

کیا آپ - رومی حروف تحجی انگریزی میں بہت سست رفتاری سے پڑھتے ہیں؟

یہ پروگرام آپ کو زیادہ تیزی سے پڑھنے میں مدد کرے گا۔ آپ نہ صرف تیزی سے پڑھ سکیں گے، بلکہ مشکل الفاظ بھی پڑھنا سیکھے جائں گے۔

آپ کو شروع کے چند یونٹ شاید بہت آسان لگیں۔ اگر ایسا ہو، تو انہیں جلدی سے کر لیں۔

نوٹ کرنے کے چند اہم نقاط

• یہ کورس آپکو انگریزی کی زبان نہیں سکھائے گا۔ یہ آپکو رومی حروف تحجی جلد اور آسانی سے پڑھنا سکھائے گا۔

• آپ کو تمام الفاظ کی سمجھ نہیں آے گی، اسکی فکر نہ کریں۔ آپ الفاظ کیسے آواز جوڑنا سیکھ رہے ہیں۔ یہ آپکی بعد میں مدد کرے گا جب آپ انگریزی زبان سیکھ رہے ہونگے۔

• الفاظ کا ترجمہ کرنے کی کوشش نہیں کریں۔ اس سے پروگرام کی ترقی بہت زیادہ سست ہو جاے گی۔

致学生

你是否还不能根据罗马字母读英文？如果你的回答是否定的，那么这个学习如何念英文的课程就是专门为你设计的。

念读英文是语言学习的基础，它会帮助你进入到课本中从而学习语言。

本教程会帮助你迈好英语学习的第一步，学习怎样用英语念读。

学习念读是一个需要花时间的过程，所以一天完成一个单元为最佳。随着整个课程的深入，你会看到自己的进步，所以不要急于求成。

你根据罗马字母读英文时速度仍然很慢吗？

本教程会帮助你看得更快。不仅仅在读的速度上，而且你还会学会如何读生涩的词汇。

你也许发现前几个单元的内容很简单。如果这样的话，你可以根据自己的程度加快学习进度。

要点提示
这项课程的目的并不是教授英语语言，而是教授怎样更快更轻松的念读罗马字母。

理解所有的词汇是不大可能的。但是不用担心，你会学会将读音和词汇结合起来。这会让你在以后学习英语时受益匪浅。

不要总想着如何把词句翻译成中文，这样做会让课程的进度变得非常缓慢。

قابل توجه دانشجویان محترم

آیا نمی توانید متون انگلیسی را که به حروف لاتین نوشته شده بخوانید؟ اگر این وضعیت را دارید، این برنامه آموزش خواندن برای شماست.

خواندن به زبان انگلیسی شرط اصلی یادگیری زبان بوده و به شما کمک می کند بتوانید از کتاب های درسی که در یادگیری زبان بسیار مفید و سودمند هستند، استفاده کنید.

این برنامه آموزش خواندن به شما کمک می کند اولین گام را در راه یادگیری زبان انگلیسی بردارید، یعنی یاد گرفتن خواندن زبان انگلیسی.

فرایند یادگیری خواندن زمان بر می باشد، بنابراین بیش از یک واحد در روز انجام ندهید. پیشرفت زمانی حاصل می شود که کل برنامه را انجام دهید، بنابراین سعی نکنید همه چیز را یک مرتبه حفظ کنید.

آیا سرعت شما در خواندن متون انگلیسی که به حروف لاتین نوشته شده کند است؟

این برنامه به شما کمک می کند سرعت خواندن خود را بالا ببرید. نه تنها خواهید آموخت که چگونه سریعتر بخوانید بلکه خواندن کلمات سخت را هم یاد خواهید گرفت.

احتمالاً چند واحد اول برایتان خیلی آسان می باشند. اگر چنین بود به سرعت آنها را به اتمام برسانید.

نکات بسیار مهم

• این دوره برای یادگیری زبان انگلیسی نمی باشد، بلکه فقط نحوه خواندن سریع و آسان الفبای لاتین را به شما آموزش خواهد داد.

• شما قادر به درک معنی همه کلمات نخواهید بود. اصلاً نگران این مسئله نباشید. شما در حال یادگیری همزمان صداها با کلمات می باشید. این کار بعداً به شما هنگام یادگیری زبان انگلیسی کمک خواهد کرد.

• سعی نکنید کلمات را ترجمه کنید. این کار سرعت پیشرفت با برنامه را خیلی کند خواهد کرد.

6

!	@	£	$	%	^	&	*	(	!	)
1	2	3	4	5	6	7	8	9	1	0

1
Read and say

1 2 3 4 5 6 7 8 9 10

10 9 8 7 6 5 4 3 2 1

- **1 3 5 7 9**
- **2 4 6 8 10**
- **8 1 7 3 5 0 9 4 10 2 6**
- **3 6 10 5 8 4 9 6 2 7 1**

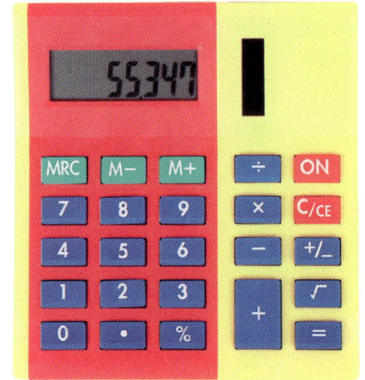

0 0 01 0123 010 0101 001

2
Read the phone numbers, then listen and check

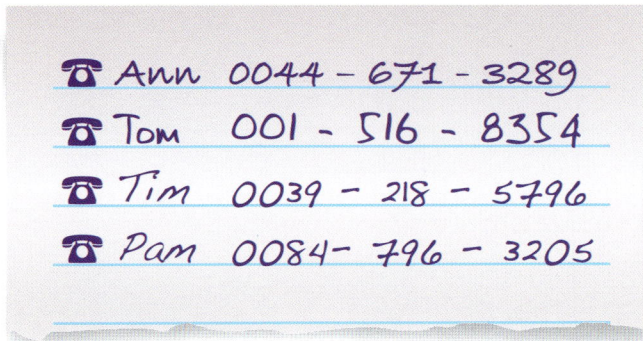

☎ Ann 0044 – 671 – 3289
☎ Tom 001 – 516 – 8354
☎ Tim 0039 – 218 – 5796
☎ Pam 0084 – 796 – 3205

3
Trace and write

1 2 3 4 5 6 7 8 9 10
1 _____ _____ _____ _____ _____ _____ _____ _____ _____

Call
911
Emergency

@
2

@ = at

① a ② t ③ i ④ n ⑤ T ⑥ I ⑦ N ⑧ A

① a ② t ③ i ④ n ⑤ T ⑥ I ⑦ A ⑧ t ⑨ N ⑩ i

① at ② it ③ an ④ in ⑤ an ⑥ at ⑦ in ⑧ it ⑨ @

① tan ② tin ③ nat ④ nit ⑤ nan ⑥ tat ⑦ TIN ⑧ NAT

① a tin ② in a tin

it ☐ tan ☐ an ① tin ☐ in ☐ @ ② nit ☐ tat ☐

at	in	✓
tin	in	
tan	tin	
it	at	

a   an   at   in   it

_____ _____ _____ _____ _____

at	an	At	@
tin	tan	*tin*	tin
it	it	**in**	IT

1
Read and say

2
Number from
1–8

3
Listen and tick

4
Trace and write

5
Find the different
word

E P

1 Read and say

1 e **2** p **3** E **4** P

1 a **2** p **3** i **4** n **5** e **6** i **7** t **8** p **9** e **10** i

1 pat **2** pen **3** pet **4** pan **5** pin **6** pit
7 pip **8** ten **9** tap **10** tip

1 at **2** pit **3** net **4** ten **5** pat **6** pet **7** nit **8** nip

pen

2 Number from 1–10

tip ☐ pit ☐ ten ☐ 1 pen ☐ pip ☐ pat ☐ pet ☐ tap ☐ pan ☐
pin ☐

3 Listen and tick

pen		pet	✓
tin		ten	
pan		pin	
net		nit	
tip		tap	

4 Trace and write

ten   pen   tap   pet   net

___ ___ ___ ___ ___

5 Read and label

ten   net   tap   PIN #   pan

1 _____ **2** _____ **3** _____ **4** _____ **5** _____

Men

11   12   13   14   15

1 2 3 4 5 6 7 8 9 10 11 12 13 14 15

2 4 6 8 10 12 14

1 3 5 7 9 11 13 15

1 m 2 d 3 M 4 D

1 m 2 d 3 t 4 p 5 D 6 a 7 i 8 n 9 M 10 e

1 dam 2 dad 3 did 4 dim 5 din 6 dip 7 mad 8 man
9 map 10 men 11 met 12 mat 13 am 14 pad

1 Dan 2 Nat 3 Ned 4 Pam 5 Ted 6 Tim

map

man		men	
mat		map	
did		dad	
mad		pad	
am		an	

man   did   am   map

did	dip	did	did
man	MAN	man	men
am	an	am	am
met	mat	met	met

1 🔊
Read and say

2 🔊
Listen and tick

3
Trace and write

4
Find the different word

5

O

1 Read and say

1 **16** 2 **17** 3 **18** 4 **19**

> •

dot

1 o 2 O

1 o 2 a 3 e 4 i 5 o 6 e 7 a 8 o 9 i 10 e
11 t 12 d 13 n 14 m 15 p 16 i 17 n 18 a 19 m

1 **on** 2 **dot** 3 **not** 4 **pot** 5 **mod** 6 **nod** 7 **pod** 8 **mop**
9 **pop** 10 **top**

1 **in** 2 **an** 3 **on** 4 **did** 5 **not** 6 **dot** 7 **pot** 8 **pat** 9 **pit**
10 **pet** 11 **tap** 12 **top** 13 **pod** 14 **Pam** 15 **Tom** 16 **mid** 17 **mod**
18 **mad**

2 Number from 1–7

dot ☐ pot ☐ not ☐1 nod ☐ top ☐ pop ☐ mod ☐

in ☐ on ☐ an ☐ it ☐ pit ☐ pot ☐ pat ☐

pot

3 Listen and tick

pod		pot	
not		nod	
Tom		Tod	
Dan		Den	
dot		top	

4 Trace and write

on   not   dot   top   pod

____   ____   ____   ____   ____

not	net	not	not
top	top	top	tap
an	on	on	on
pot	dot	dot	dot

e-mail address book

Pam	Pam@pop.net
Tom	Tom@pen.net
Dan	Dan@nat.net
Ted	Ted16@top.net
Tod	Tod12@map.net
Tim	Tim19@pit.net

Pam@pop.net	Pam at pop dot net
Tom@pen.net	Tom at pen dot net
Dan@nat.net	Dan at nat dot net
Ted16@top.net	Ted 16 at top dot net
Tod12@map.net	Tod 12 at map dot net
Tim19@pit.net	Tim 19 at pit dot net

atpenmaptennot	at pen map ten not
potnotdotpodmoptop	
dippinpittiptinmid	
tenmenpendenmet	
panmadtanpadmat	

top

6

1
Read and say

■ 20 21 22 23 24 25

**■ 1 2 3 4 5 6 7 8 9 10
11 12 13 14 15 16 17 18
19 20 21 22 23 24 25**

van

1 **g** 2 *g* 3 **G** 4 **v** 5 **V**

1 g 2 v 3 t 4 d 5 v 6 m 7 *g* 8 p 9 n 10 g 11 v 12 e 13 i 14 o 15 a

1 **dig** 2 **dog** 3 **get** 4 **God** 5 **got** 6 **peg** 7 **nag** 8 **tag** 9 **van** 10 **vat** 11 **vet** 12 **vim**

1 **dig** 2 **did** 3 **vim** 4 **dog** 5 **got** 6 **God** 7 **get** 8 **gig** 9 **peg** 10 **vat** 11 **tan** 12 **tag** 13 **van** 14 **man** 15 **met** 16 **vet** 17 **ten** 18 **nag** 19 **Dan** 20 **Tom**

2
Number from 1–11

tag ☐ peg ☐ dig ☐1 dog ☐ got ☐ get ☐ God ☐ vat ☐ vet ☐
van ☐ vim ☐

3
Listen and tick

got		get	
God		got	
vet		get	
man		van	
vim		dim	
dig		gig	
nab		nag	

dog

4
Trace and write

get   got   van   vet
___   ___   ___   ___

get	*get*	got	get
did	dig	did	*did*
van	nan	van	*van*
pet	*vet*	*VET*	vet
got	got	**got**	*not*

atpenmaptennot — *at pen map ten not*

gotgetdogpegtagdigpig

vanvatvetvim

dogdimdiddotdam

podpitpenpatpigpotpin

tentantintagtoptan

menmanmopmodmatmap

notnagnetnodnipnap

inonamanit

■ a am an at did in it get got not on
■ GET IN NOT AM DID AT GOT ON IT A AN
■ *got a not an it am on in get at did*
■ AM NOT AT GET ON GOT DID A IT IN AN

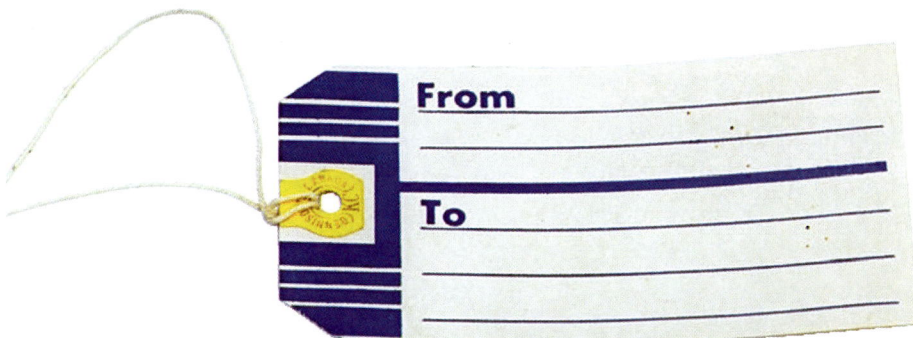

From

To

tag

15

H   L

1 *h*   2 **H**   3 **l**   4 *l*   5 **L**

1 *h*   2 **l**   3 *v*   4 **d**   5 **p**   6 *m*   7 **g**   8 **n**
9 **t**   10 **i**   11 **e**   12 **a**   13 *o*   14 *L*   15 **H**   16 M
17 **G**   18 *V*   19 T   20 *P*   21 **D**

hat

1 **had**   2 **hat**   3 **hen**   4 **hid**   5 **him**   6 **hit**   7 **hot**   8 **hop**
9 **lap**   10 **let**   11 **lid**   12 **lip**   13 **log**   14 **lot**   15 **hal**   16 **halal**

1 **lot**   2 **had**   3 **log**   4 **him**   5 **let**   6 **lip**   7 **hot**   8 **hen**   9 **lap**
10 **hit**   11 **lop**   12 **hat**   13 **hid**   14 **lid**   15 **got**   16 **van**   17 **vet**   18 **did**
19 **top**   20 **lad**   21 **lit**   22 **mat**   23 **hip**   24 **hop**   25 **tip**

let ☐   lad [1]   lap ☐   lot ☐   lid ☐   lip ☐   log ☐

hen ☐   him ☐   hot ☐   hit ☐   hat ☐   had ☐   hid ☐

let		lot		him		hit	
had		lad		hen		ten	
log		lot		lad		mad	
had		hat		lip		lap	
dim		him		vet		let	

let   lot   had   him   hot

___   ___   ___   ___   ___

a laptop   a hot tap   a pot, a lid on top

1 _____   2 _____   3 _____

5
Read and label

- a top / a lap / a laptop
- a tap / a hot tap
- a pot / a hot pot / a lid / on top / a pot, a lid on top
- a hot pot, a lid on top
- log / log on / log on a laptop
- let / let him / let him in / get him / get him a laptop

6
Read, then listen and check

- a had let him did not had vat in it got lot
- GET HIM AN NOT ON GOT AM IN DID IT AT
- did got get let on in an lot him had at it
- HIM LET NOT HAD A GOT DID GET LOT LET AT IT

7
Read key words

M	H	A	D	O	V	D	E
L	I	P	A	H	I	T	L
A	M	E	I	D	M	L	O
P	T	G	L	O	T	A	G
N	D	T	E	G	N	D	M
V	I	G	T	V	A	N	V
L	G	M	A	V	G	D	E
T	D	P	H	O	P	L	T

hen

8
Find words from Units 6 and 7

8

U C

1
Read and say

[1] u [2] U [3] c [4] C

up

[1] u [2] c [3] a [4] i [5] u [6] o [7] u [8] e [9] c [10] t [11] d [12] c [13] v [14] C [15] G [16] T [17] G [18] C [19] U [20] O

[1] up [2] can [3] cap [4] cat [5] cog [6] cot [7] cup [8] cut [9] gum [10] gun [11] hug [12] hut [13] mud [14] mug [15] nut

[1] pop [2] pup [3] can [4] cap [5] hog [6] hug [7] vat [8] cat [9] gum [10] up [11] mug [12] mud [13] not [14] nut [15] hut [16] hot [17] tug [18] cut [19] cup [20] cop

2
Number from 1–7

mug ☐ gum ☐ mud ☐ hug [1] cog [2] hut ☐ nut ☐

cup ☐ up ☐ cot ☐ cat ☐ cap ☐ can ☐ cut ☐

3
Listen and tick

pop		pup		hog		hut	
cap		cat		mud		mug	
hug		hog		op		up	
gum		gun		cup		cut	
tug		tag		cot		cut	
not		nut		hut		hug	
top up		tip up		pop up		top up	

4
Trace and write

nut   can   gum   cup   mug

_____ _____ _____ _____ _____

5
Read and label

mug   nut   cup   gum   tin

[1] _____ [2] _____ [3] _____ [4] _____ [5] _____

cup   CAT   top-up   gum

2010 FIFA World Cup
South Africa™

can	CAN	can	cat	can
TOP-UP	top-up	tip-up	Top-up	Top-Up
mug	MUG	mug	gum	Mug
hut	nut	NUT	Nut	nut
Cup	CUP	Cup	cup	cap

atpenmaptennot   *at pen map ten not*

cancapcopcutcogcup   _____

mugmadmenmapmid   _____

dogdimdendamdan   _____

hadhimhathothughut   _____

▪ can   up   did   had   not   got   lot   him   let
▪ GET   DID   HIM   CAN   ON   IN   UP   IT   GOT
▪ AN   IN   ON   UP   GOT   HIM   CAN   LOT   LET   DID
▪ at   am   in   it   up   get   can   got   get   did   let   up   can

hug

cut

9

| B | S |

1 Read and say

1 b **2** B **3** s **4** S

bus

1 b **2** c **3** d **4** p **5** s **6** v **7** g **8** t **9** s **10** b **11** h **12** l **13** m **14** B **15** G **16** S **17** H **18** S **19** V **20** B **21** L

1 us **2** bad **3** bag **4** bed **5** beg **6** big **7** bin **8** bit **9** bug **10** bun **11** bus **12** but **13** sad **14** set **15** sip **16** sit **17** sum **18** sun **19** cub **20** hub **21** tub

1 hut **2** but **3** sit **4** sat **5** set **6** bug **7** hug **8** us **9** up **10** Sam **11** bun **12** sum **13** bed **14** gun **15** bug **16** sad **17** bad **18** bin **19** bib **20** bag **21** beg **22** sin **23** SIM **24** sub **25** bus **26** hub **27** bit

2 Number from 1–7

bug ☐ big ☐ tug ☐ mug [1] gun ☐ sag ☐ sad ☐

bus ☐ us ☐ sub ☐ sun ☐ sum ☐ sin ☐ Sid ☐

3 Listen and tick

bad		bud		sun		sum	
sad		Sid		set		sat	
big		bid		sin		sun	
bat		bad		bed		Ted	
us		up		tub		cub	

4 Trace and write

us   bus   but   big   bad   bit

5 Read and label

bag   bug   bed   sat nav   SIM

1 _____ **2** _____ **3** _____ **4** _____ **5** _____

20

sun	sum	sum	sum
but	**but**	bit	but
bad	bad	bed	bad
sad	sap	SAD	sad
bug	big	big	big

6
Find the different word

atpenmaptennot — *at pen map ten not*

binbagbegbudbugbusbut

sitsunsadsetsumsip

gungotgumget

bussunbuttugtap

7
Separate the words

sunset

Meg Tom Dan Ted Pam Bob Sam Seb Hal Vic Peg
Deb Sal Bill Moll Ann Cab Mac Pat Tim Dot Nat

8
Read the names

Dan@mac.com   Dan   at   mac   dot   com
Bill@pop.net   Bill   at   pop   dot   net

9
Read and say the e-mail addresses, then listen and check

```
e-mail address book

Dan    Dan@mac.com
Bill   Bill@pop.net
Seb    Seb@sun.com
Vic    Vic@van.net
Sal    Sal@mac.com
Sam    Sam@big.bus.net
```

on a bus	but not us	get up	it did	dot com
in a bus	but not him	get on	get dim sum	sunset

10
Read, then listen and check

21

10 R

red bus

1 r 2 **R** 3 r 4 **R**

1 r 2 s 3 c 4 d 5 v 6 m 7 g 8 b
9 t 10 l 11 m 12 h 13 r 14 **G** 15 **R** 16 **V**
17 **H** 18 **S** 19 **B** 20 **P** 21 **L**

1 **rag** 2 **ram** 3 **ran** 4 **rap** 5 **rat** 6 **red** 7 **rep** 8 **rib** 9 **rid**
10 **rig** 11 **rim** 12 **rip** 13 **rob** 14 **rod** 15 **Ron** 16 **rub** 17 **rug** 18 **run**
19 **rut** 20 **Arab**

1 **rag** 2 **bug** 3 **bag** 4 **rim** 5 **rot** 6 **rub** 7 **Rod** 8 **rat** 9 **rut**
10 **rip** 11 **rap** 12 **rig** 13 **rug** 14 **rid** 15 **red** 16 **ram** 17 **ran** 18 **run**
19 **Arab** 20 **Ron**

rat ☐ red ☐1 rid ☐ rob ☐ rub ☐ rib ☐ rep ☐

rib		rip		lot		rot	
rag		rug		rip		lip	
rat		vat		rap		lab	
rot		rat		rut		hut	
led		red		vet		red	

red   run   ran   rip

____   ____   ____   ____

rug   red   run   rag   rat

1 _____   2 _____   3 _____   4 _____   5 _____

Ron   Rob   Rod   Ric   Bob   Mac   Sal   Seb

big pen	bad pun	big bag	red rug
red bus	hot sun	bad pet	red rag
big bug	sad man	red pen	rat run

Arab
Abbas
Arabic

RAM	RAM	ROM	RAM
red	red	red	rod
run	ran	run	run
rid	rib	rib	rib

R	O	B	H	T	L	N	R
A	V	U	R	I	P	S	O
M	H	S	A	D	R	E	D
P	S	U	N	B	I	T	R
R	A	G	S	U	M	C	E
G	U	R	A	T	V	R	P
E	S	I	L	G	P	U	B
B	U	G	C	N	H	T	U

2 GB RAM

CD-ROM

red rug

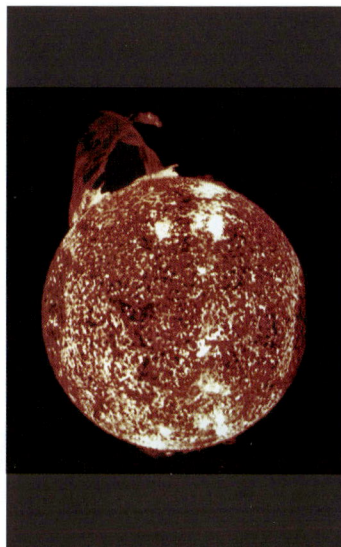
hot sun

Burj Al-Arab

6
Read the names

7
Read, then listen and check

8
Find the different word

9
Find words from Units 9 and 10

23

11

Y W J

a jet

1 Read and say

1 y 2 w 3 j 4 Y 5 W 6 J

1 y 2 w 3 s 4 w 5 v 6 y 7 j 8 g 9 b
10 p 11 n 12 m 13 w 14 Y 15 V 16 W 17 G
18 J 19 Y 20 W 21 J

1 yen 2 yes 3 yet 4 yob 5 web 6 wed
7 wet 8 win 9 wit 10 jab 11 jam 12 jet 13 jig
14 job 15 jug 16 Japan

1 yet 2 jet 3 yob 4 job 5 yes 6 rug 7 jug 8 jig 9 win
10 web 11 wet 12 vet 13 yen 14 van 15 jab 16 lab 17 Sam
18 jam 19 Japan 20 Jim 21 Jan 22 Jen

2 Number from 1–7

yes ☐ jet ☐ yen ☐ yet ☐ job 1 yam ☐ jam ☐

win ☐ wet ☐ web ☐ wit ☐ job ☐ jig ☐ jug ☐

3 Listen and tick

jet		yet		jig		jug	
yob		job		jam		yam	
yet		wet		yes		yen	
jet		wet		web		wet	
yet		wet		Jen		Jan	

4 Trace and write

yes   yet   job   win   wet

_____ _____ _____ _____ _____

5 Read and label

jug   jam   wet   yen

1 _____ 2 _____ 3 _____ 4 _____

24

6
Find the different word

yes	yet	yes	*YES*
job	job	job	job
win	win	vim	win
jab	lab	*lab*	lab

Jim Jan Hal Dot Al Meg Len Ben Val Jen Win

7
Read the names

8
Read, then listen and check

Jap ● an
Japan

Mad ● rid
Madrid

Bas ● ra
Basra

Leb ● an ● on
Lebanon

Can ● a ● da
Canada

Arab ● ic
Arabic

Japan   Madrid   Basra   Lebanon   Canada   Arabic

yes, yes, yes	a JAL jet	win yen	tin can
but not yet	not us	yen in Japan	web jam
747 jet	a job in Japan	wed him	get a lot

atpenmaptennot   *at   pen   map   ten   not*

jetjamjobjigjabjug

webwitwetwedwin

yobyesyetyenyes

ranridredrimrubrug

9
Separate the words

25

12

F X Z

1 Read and say

[1] f [2] x [3] z [4] F [5] X [6] Z

box

[1] f [2] x [3] z [4] s [5] v [6] f [7] x [8] s [9] g [10] j [11] f [12] w [13] y [14] S [15] X [16] W [17] F [18] J [19] Z [20] G [21] V

[1] fan [2] fat [3] fed [4] fig [5] fit [6] fix [7] fizz [8] jazz [9] fox [10] fog [11] fun [12] if [13] box [14] sex [15] six [16] wax [17] tax [18] mix [19] fax [20] zigzag [21] exam [22] exit [23] ox [24] Oz

[1] fox [2] mix [3] tax [4] sax [5] six [6] sex [7] fax [8] fit [9] exam [10] fat [11] fun [12] if [13] wax [14] fan [15] zed [16] exit [17] zigzag [18] fig [19] jazz [20] box [21] fizz [22] fix

2 Number from 1–7

fizz ☐ fix ☐ six [1] box ☐ exit ☐ exam ☐ jazz ☐

if ☐ zigzag ☐ fog ☐ fit ☐ fat ☐ fan ☐ fun ☐

3 Listen and tick

tax		wax		fig		fog	
fax		fox		jazz		fizz	
fan		fun		ox		Oz	
sip		six		six		sax	
fizz		fix		fin		fun	

4 Trace and write

if   six   fax   zigzag   jazz

___ ___ ___ ___ ___

5 Read and label

fan   sax   zigzag   fox   six

[1] _____ [2] _____ [3] _____ [4] _____ [5] _____

@   web   RAM   rom   dot com   net   fax   box

ex • it

exit

Fed • Ex

FedEx

EXX • ON

EXXON

zig • zag

zigzag

Tex • a • co

Texaco

LEX • US

LEXUS

Sam Cox

Exco Inc
PO Box 659
Dallas, Texas
TX 345812

Tel: 214 5091 487
Fax: 214 5091 763
e-mail: sam.cox@exco.net   web: www.exco.com

K C K

sock

1 Read and say

①k ②K ③c ④ck

①k ②ck ③c ④s ⑤z ⑥x ⑦g ⑧j ⑨v ⑩w ⑪b ⑫p ⑬y ⑭j ⑮C ⑯K ⑰X ⑱R ⑲T ⑳K ㉑S

①keg ②kid ③kin ④kit ⑤kick ⑥back ⑦deck ⑧dock ⑨duck ⑩lick ⑪lock ⑫luck ⑬pack ⑭pick ⑮rock ⑯sack ⑰sick ⑱sock ⑲tick ⑳wick

①rock ②pick ③back ④pack ⑤sack ⑥kid ⑦kit ⑧duck ⑨dock ⑩deck ⑪luck ⑫lack ⑬lick ⑭sick ⑮tick ⑯sock ⑰kin ⑱keg ⑲wick ⑳kick ㉑lock ㉒muck ㉓rack ㉔backpack

2 Number from 1–7

back ☐   deck [1]   lock ☐   rock ☐   luck ☐   tick ☐   kick ☐

3 Listen and tick

six		sick		pat		pack	
tip		tick		Mick		mix	
kick		wick		tack		tax	
bag		back		rack		rock	
sat		sack		lock		luck	
sit		six		dock		duck	
fit		fix		kick		kit	

4 Trace and write

kit   back   kick   rock

_____   _____   _____   _____

5 Read and label

lock   sack   backpack   duck   rock

①_____   ②_____   ③_____   ④_____   ⑤_____

tick tock... tick tock...
tick tock...

a am an at @ bit but
can did had him if in
it get got let lot not
on up us yes

Nick   Jack   Mick   Rick   Rex   Tex   Dick

padlock

backpack   bad luck   pick a lock   a bad back
tick box   big pack   dock deck   tick tock
kick-box   red rock   a sick duck   padlock

atpenmaptennot   *at pen map ten not*

kicklockpackbackluck   _____

kidkinkitkickkidkick   _____

fizzzedjazzzen   _____

sixfaxboxsexfixtaxwax   _____

J	E	X	I	T	A	X	F
B	O	X	W	I	F	I	G
Z	J	R	I	C	I	F	L
F	S	O	C	K	X	P	U
A	J	C	K	I	L	A	C
X	A	K	X	D	O	C	K
F	Z	J	K	I	C	K	E
J	Z	E	P	C	K	Z	G

2 Jazz
Rap
Hiphop

1 Rock
Metal
Pop

kick-box

6
Read the key
words at speed

7
Read the names

8
Read, then listen
and check

9
Separate the
words

10
Find words from
Units 12 and 13

Q	U	T	H	W	H

File   Tools   Help
About
Open File
Online Registration

Preferences
Services
Edit
Quit   = Q

quit

1 Read and say

1 **qu** 2 **th** 3 **wh** 4 **Qu** 5 **Th**
6 **Wh**

1 **qu** 2 **k** 3 **c** 4 **ck** 5 **qu** 6 **t** 7 **th** 8 **wh**
9 **w** 10 **qu** 11 **th** 12 **Qu** 13 **Th** 14 **Wh** 15 **C**
16 **Qu** 17 **Th**

1 **quid** 2 **quip** 3 **quit** 4 **quick**
5 **than** 6 **that** 7 **them** 8 **then** 9 **this**
10 **when** 11 **whim** 12 **whip** 13 **whiz** 14 **with**

1 **quip** 2 **whip** 3 **this** 4 **with** 5 **them** 6 **then** 7 **quid**
8 **quick** 9 **that** 10 **hat** 11 **this** 12 **win** 13 **whim** 14 **whiz**
15 **with** 16 **wit** 17 **wick**

2 Number from 1–7

when ☐   then ☐ 1   quit ☐   whip ☐   quick ☐   this ☐   with ☐

3 Listen and tick

quit		quick		quip		quid	
when		then		wit		with	
then		them		quick		kick	
with		whiz		quid		kid	
than		then		quit		kit	
win		whim		this		fizz	

4 Trace and write

this   that   when   with   quick

_____ _____ _____ _____ _____

5 Find the different word

when	WHEN	when	then
that	than	that	that
quick	quick	quick	quit
then	them	them	them

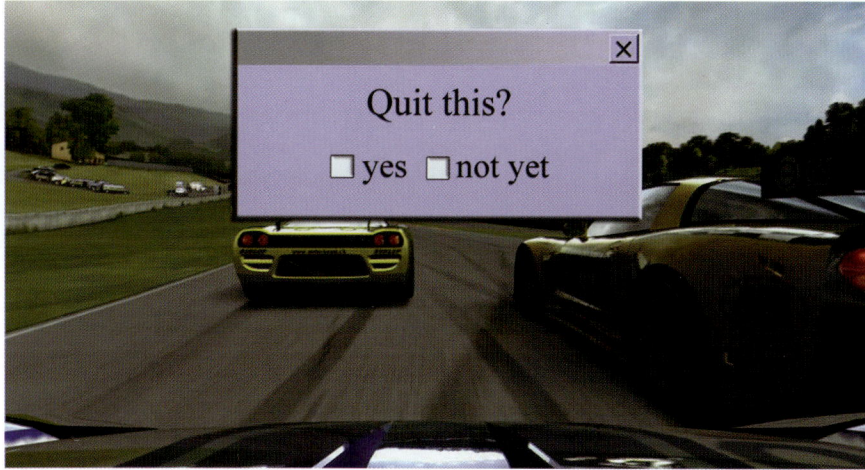

6
Read, then listen
and check

Quit   Quick   *When*   *Quick*   Quick   When

quip   that   *them*   **when**   quick   *this*   get   *got*

with   than   but   bit   can   did   *quick*   quit

then   when   quip   *quit*   *Quick*   this   whip

7
Separate the
words

quitquickquip   *quit quick quip*

whenthenthemthanwinwith

whimwitwithwhen

quitwhenquidthemthanthen

8
Find words from
Unit 14

Q	U	I	T	S	G	U	Z
U	F	T	H	E	N	W	H
I	Q	U	I	P	W	H	K
C	U	C	S	W	H	I	P
K	I	B	W	H	E	Z	K
J	D	T	H	A	N	E	J
F	X	W	I	T	H	A	T
T	H	E	M	D	V	A	L

tick

15 | S H · C H · T C H

S H C H T C H

1 Read and say

1 sh 2 ch 3 tch 4 Sh 5 Ch

1 sh 2 ch 3 c 4 ck 5 s 6 sh 7 qu 8 wh
9 j 10 tch 11 y 12 Th 13 Ch 14 Sh 15 C 16 S
17 J

fish and chips

1 shed 2 ship 3 shop 4 shot 5 shock
6 shut 7 chap 8 chat 9 chin 10 chip
11 chop 12 cash 13 dash 14 dish 15 fish
16 posh 17 wish 18 much 19 such 20 which
21 itch 22 catch 23 match 24 patch

1 ship 2 chip 3 shop 4 chop 5 wish 6 which 7 cash
8 catch 9 posh 10 patch 11 dash 12 match 13 dish 14 shed
15 much 16 such 17 shut 18 chat 19 chin 20 shock 21 itch
22 pitch 23 ditch 24 fetch

2 Number from 1–7

shed ☐ shut ☐ shop ☐1 ship ☐ wish ☐ dash ☐ cash ☐

chat ☐ chop ☐ chin ☐ which ☐ much ☐ catch ☐ fetch ☐

3 Listen and tick

ship		chip		mash		match	
shin		chin		lash		latch	
shop		chop		cash		catch	
shock		chock		dish		ditch	
wish		dish		itch		which	
mush		much		sash		hatch	
hush		such		itch		fetch	

4 Trace and write

shop   much   which   wish   cash

_____ _____ _____ _____ _____

5 Read and label

dish   match   shop   ship   chips

1 _____ 2 _____ 3 _____ 4 _____ 5 _____

and   AND   &   **and**   &   and   And   &   and   &

and	&
fish	which
chips	shop
shop	Which shop?
fish shop	Which man?
chip shop	Which box?
fish & chips	Which ship?
fish and chip shop	And which dish?
Which fish shop?	Which fish and chip shop?

To the SHOPS

FISH & CHIPS RESTAURANT

and	&	ant	and
much	mush	much	much
which	which	WHICH	hitch
shop	ship	ship	ship
cash	catch	cash	cash

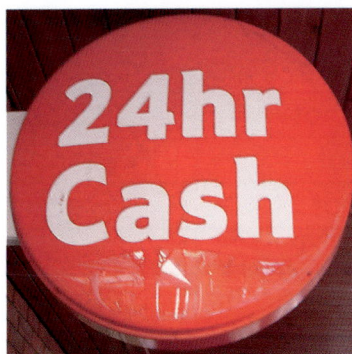

24hr Cash

W	M	X	A	N	D	R	C
H	U	S	H	E	D	J	A
I	C	H	S	H	I	P	T
C	H	O	P	J	S	C	C
H	G	P	O	S	H	H	H
C	A	S	H	X	Z	I	W
Z	M	A	T	C	H	P	Y
S	H	O	C	K	Q	U	K

THE SHIP INN

FISH & CHIPS

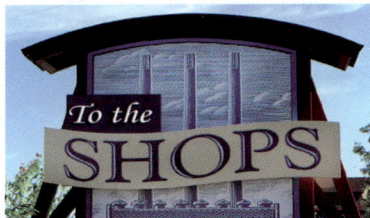

6
Read, then listen and check

7
Find the different word

8
Find words from Unit 15

16

o o

1 o **2** oo **3** O **4** Oo

1 o **2** oo **3** a **4** e **5** i **6** u **7** qu **8** oo **9** e **10** o

moon

1 lot **2** loot **3** shot **4** shoot **5** rot **6** root **7** zoo **8** zoom

1 boo **2** boot **3** food **4** loo **5** moon **6** noon **7** roof **8** room **9** root **10** shoot **11** soon **12** too **13** zoo **14** zoom

not ☐ noon ☐ hot |1| hoot ☐ too ☐ tot ☐ shoot ☐

shot		shoot		zoo		zoom	
lot		loot		loo		loot	
rot		root		boo		boot	
sock		soon		rom		room	
hot		hoot		roof		root	
posh		patch		moo		moon	
fox		fetch		chat		shoot	

too   food   soon   room

_____ _____ _____ _____

zoom   boot   food   roof   noon

1_____ **2**_____ **3**_____ **4**_____ **5**_____

6
Read, then listen and check

1 boo **2** do **3** you **4** too **5** you **6** do **7** zoo

boo!	Oo!	not soon
boo hoo	hot food	hot at noon
boom boom	bedroom	Do you?
root toot toot	rooftop	too soon
whoosh boom	back room	you do

a am an and & at @ bit but can did had do
him if in it get got let lot much not on room
shop soon than that them this too up us when
which with yes you

7
Read the key words at speed

toot   moo   whoosh   boo hoo   hoot   boom

8
Find the words

boo hoo!

BOOM

moo

hoot

toot

whoosh

17 E E E A

COFFEE SHOP *and* TEA ROOMS
Entrance in Market Place

1 e 2 ee 3 e 4 ea

1 e 2 oo 3 ee 4 o 5 ea 6 e 7 u 8 i
9 Ee 10 Ea

1 **ben** 2 **been** 3 **bean** 4 **ten** 5 **teen**
6 **team**

1 **bee** 2 **beef** 3 **been** 4 **feet** 5 **keep** 6 **meet** 7 **see**
8 **seem** 9 **seen** 10 **sheep** 11 **week** 12 **coffee** 13 **cheek**
14 **queen** 15 **tea** 16 **sea** 17 **eat** 18 **each** 19 **beach** 20 **read**
21 **cheap** 22 **meat** 23 **seat** 24 **wheat** 25 **teach**

bee ☐ beat ☐ fee ☐ feet ☐ wheat ☐ queen ☐ 1 been ☐

fed		feed		Ken		keen	
check		cheek		keen		queen	
red		read		eat		each	
met		meat		beak		beach	
wet		wheat		tea		teach	
set		seat		eel		wheel	
net		neat		sheep		ship	

read   each   been   see   sea

___   ___   ___   ___   ___

feet   sheep   tea   seat   meat

   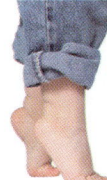 

1 _____ 2 _____ 3 _____ 4 _____ 5 _____

pee	5p	10p	15p	20p	25p

20	30	40	50	60	70	80	90
20p	30p	40p	50p	60p	70p	80p	90p

Eat at …

POOLE BEACH COFFEE SHOP

<u>This week</u>

| CUP OF HOT TEA | .... | 1.40 |
| MUG OF COFFEE | .... | 1.70 |

<u>Salads</u>

BEEF	....	4.50
EGG	....	3.80
CHEESE	....	3.90
FISH	....	5.30
EGG WITH CHEESE	....	6.20

+ VAT @ 15%

coffee

cheese

Dick Bean
Dee Boon
Viv Booth
Mick Cash
Ben Chan
Jim Choo
Liz Cox
Adam Dean

Sam Doon
Ann Fox
Quentin Hancock
Hal Keen
Dan Lee
Bob Moon
Jack Nash
Nick Read
Jan Seed

6 🔴
Read, then listen and check

7 🔴
Read the menu aloud, then listen and check

8 🔴
Read the names

B E M E

1
Read and say

1 **bed** 2 **bee** 3 **beat** 4 **be**

1 **be** 2 **he** 3 **me** 4 **she** 5 **we**

bee

1 **be** 2 **bet** 3 **been** 4 **beat**
5 **me** 6 **men** 7 **meet** 8 **mean**
9 **he** 10 **hen** 11 **heel** 12 **heat**
13 **she** 14 **shed** 15 **sheep**
16 **we** 17 **when** 18 **weep** 19 **wheat** 20 **wheel**

1 **meet** 2 **me** 3 **met** 4 **mean** 5 **men** 6 **wheat** 7 **wet**
8 **we** 9 **when** 10 **weep** 11 **sheet** 12 **shed** 13 **she** 14 **sea**
15 **heap** 16 **heel** 17 **hem** 18 **he** 19 **hen** 20 **Ben** 21 **been**
22 **be** 23 **bee** 24 **beach** 25 **wheel**

2
Number from
1–7

he ☐ she ☐ heat ☐ sheep ☐ when ☐ hen ☐ we [1]

me ☐ men ☐ mean ☐ bet ☐ beat ☐ be ☐ been ☐

3
Listen and tick

me		meat		sea		she	
met		meet		set		sheet	
beat		be		seat		seem	
Ben		been		he		heat	
each		beach		when		hen	
wheat		wet		heel		wheel	
we		week		he and she		she and he	

4
Trace and write

be   me   we   he   she

____   ____   ____   ____   ____

5
Find the different
word

be	BE	he	be	Be
The	the	the	the	then
she	she	she	sea	she
we	Wii	WE	We	we
he	HE	he	the	He

Top 100 words in English:

#1 the   #2 be   #16 he   #27 we   #30 she   #50 me   #69 see

The Manchester United football team are in the United Arab Emirates today. They arrived at the Dubai International Airport on a British Airways flight, and went to the Shangri-La Hotel for lunch. The team are playing this evening against the national team at the Al-Rashid Stadium. The match begins at 8 p.m. The referee is from the People's Republic of China. The stadium will be full for the match.

1 the   2 The   3 and   4 And   5 then   6 tea   7 the   8 he   9 &   10 @

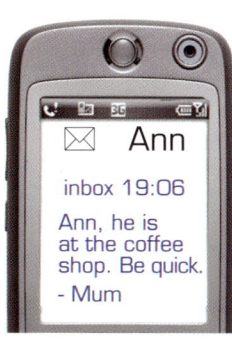

Ann

inbox 16:33

Meet me at six.
- Josh

Josh

inbox 16:35

Be at the bus stop at seven.
- Ann

Ann

inbox 16:45

When? Seven not six?
- Josh

Josh

inbox 16:52

Yes, you meet me at seven.
- Ann

Viv

INBOX 19:01

Viv, I am at the coffee shop. Ann is not.
- Josh

Josh

inbox 19:05

Ann is at the bus stop.
- Viv

Ann

inbox 19:06

Ann, he is at the coffee shop. Be quick.
- Mum

Viv

INBOX 19:12

We (Josh & I) met at the coffee shop.
- Ann

6
Look

7
Highlight *the* in the text

8
Read, then listen and check

9
Read the text messages, then listen and check

19   A Y A I

RAILWAY 1

1
Read and say

1 **a**   2 **ay**   3 **ai**   4 **AY**   5 **AI**

1 **o**   2 **a**   3 **e**   4 **i**   5 **u**   6 **oo**   7 **ee**   8 **ea**
9 **ay**   10 **ai**   11 **a**   12 **ea**   13 **ai**   14 **a**   15 **ay**   16 **oo**
17 **o**   18 **u**

1 **pan**   2 **pain**   3 **pay**   4 **Hal**   5 **hail**   6 **hay**

1 **bay**   2 **day**   3 **gay**   4 **hay**   5 **jay**   6 **lay**   7 **may**   8 **pay**
9 **ray**   10 **say**   11 **way**   12 **aid**   13 **chain**   14 **fail**   15 **jail**   16 **laid**
17 **mail**   18 **main**   19 **nail**   20 **pain**   21 **rail**   22 **sail**   23 **tail**
24 **wait**   25 **aim**

2
Number from
1–7

may ☐   day ☐   mail ☐   rail ☐   way ☐   wait [1]   pay ☐

3
Listen and tick

man		main		say		sail	
way		wait		may		main	
Dan		day		ray		rain	
nail		mail		pay		paid	
wail		wait		lay		laid	

4
Trace and write

say   day   way   wait   mail

_____   _____   _____   _____   _____

5
Read and label

mailbox   pay   chain   hay   May

1 _____   2 _____   3 _____   4 _____   5 _____

| A | Y | A | I |

WAY IN

U.S.MAIL

RAIL CROSSING WAY

6
Read, say and check

1 got 2 soon 3 wet 4 we 5 weep 6 wheat 7 mad 8 may 9 mail

10 chat 11 chain 12 sail 13 say 14 sack 15 aim 16 aid 17 paid 18 gain

19 gay 20 gap 21 wail 22 way 23 rain

e-mail	railway	May Day	get paid
mailbox	pay me	payday	pay soon
chat room	way in	wait in	rain hat

7
Read, then listen and check

8
Find and circle all the words with *ay*/ *ai*

⊙ **Main disc**   ▣ **Mailbox**   🗩 **Chat room**   🌐 **Internet**   🗓 **May 23**

INBOX … e-mails

Dan@quick.net	Good day …	May 21 08:30
Jay@UK.rail.com	railway tickets	May 21 09:15
Quentin.Cox@cashbox.net	pay - be quick	May 22 10:45
Gail@goon.net	see me this week	May 23 00:30
Doc.Nash@bigmoon.co.uk	this way to cheap pills	May 23 07:24
Ben.Pain@hotmail.com	e-mail me soon	May 23 09:37
Jan@away.day.co.uk	Jack is away that day	May 23 11:51

THIS WAY →

PAY ↓

MAILBOX

N O O A ~ O E .

OPEN 7 DAYS A WEEK

1 Read and say

1 o 2 oo 3 a 4 ay 5 ai
6 e 7 ee 8 ea 9 oa 10 oe

1 got 2 go 3 no 4 so 5 Jo
6 goat 7 toe

1 oat 2 boat 3 coat 4 coach 5 foam 6 goat 7 load
8 loan 9 moan 10 road 11 roam 12 soak 13 soap 14 doe
15 foe 16 Joe 17 toe 18 woe 19 open

1 goat 2 got 3 go 4 fog 5 foe 6 food 7 main 8 moan
9 mail 10 sock 11 soak 12 soap 13 cop 14 coat 15 coach
16 rod 17 road 18 raid 19 reed 20 read 21 say 22 so 23 sea
24 see 25 sob

2 Number from 1–7

no ☐ toe ☐1 so ☐ soap ☐ boat ☐ foe ☐ open ☐

3 Listen and tick

got		goat		coat		coach	
man		moan		doe		Joe	
rod		road		a pen		open	
rom		roam		so		sob	
cot		coat		go		got	

4 Trace and write

no   so   go   road   toe

_____ _____ _____ _____ _____

5 Read and label

coach   coat   boat   goat   soap

1 _____ 2 _____ 3 _____ 4 _____ 5 _____

01-202-3456   020-709-0430

1 **no** **2** **do** **3** **don't** **4** **open** **5** **woe** **6** **won't**
7 **the** **8** **open** **9** **you** **10** **don't** **11** **won't**

No way!	no soap	big toe	won't go
Go this way	no coat	don't eat that	won't get
soap dish	no road	don't go	won't say
hand soap	no coach	don't say no	won't see

No dogs

NO EXIT

Shell Bay OPEN

coats

coach stop

ROAD OPEN

Q	C	S	O	G	J	N	U
R	O	A	D	O	T	O	E
X	A	M	O	A	N	Z	S
O	C	O	A	T	B	G	O
A	H	P	B	V	O	X	A
T	F	E	S	O	A	P	K
H	W	N	Q	Y	T	Q	L
A	F	O	A	M	W	O	E

SOAP

43

21 A R

1 a 2 ai 3 ay 4 **ar** 5 o 6 oo

7 e 8 ee 9 ea 10 oa 11 oe 12 **ar**

TO CAR → PARK

1 cat 2 **car** 3 fan 4 f**ar** 5 am 6 **ar**m

7 pat 8 p**ar**t

1 bar 2 car 3 far 4 jar 5 arc 6 arm 7 art

1 bark 2 card 3 charm 4 chart 5 dark 6 farm 7 harm

8 hard 9 bard 10 lark 11 mark 12 park 13 part 14 tart

car [1] art ☐ cart ☐ far ☐ arm ☐ farm ☐ park ☐

chat		chart		bark		dark	
bad		bard		harm		charm	
pack		park		car		card	
lack		lark		far		farm	
had		hard		art		part	
jam		jar		arc		mark	

car   far   arm   park   card

P Beach car park →

cart   card   car   jar   arm

1 _____ 2 _____ 3 _____ 4 _____ 5 _____

Beach Road   Farm Traffic   Red Card   Art
Coffee Bar   Park Mark

paycarpark   *pay   car   park*

hardmarkdarklark   _____

farmharmcharmtart   _____

jararmartpartarc   _____

beachroadcarpark   _____

a   am   an   and   &   at   @   be   been   bit   but   can
day   did   do   don't   each   eat   get   go   got   had
he   him   if   in   it   let   lot   may   me   mean   much
no   not   on   read   room   say   see   seen   she   shop
so   soon   than   that   the   them   this   too   up   us
we   when   which   with   won't   yes   you

car park	red card	part six	beach car park
coach park	art card	ten marks	sheep farm
pay and park	coffee bar	top mark	goat farm
bad arm	tea bar	jam jar	dark day

1 _____ 2 _____ 3 _____ 4 _____ 5 _____

S T ~ ~ S T

1 s 2 t 3 st 4 b 5 ch 6 sh
7 s 8 ck 9 qu 10 st

1 **star** 2 **start** 3 **stay** 4 **best**
5 **just** 6 **must**

STOP

1 stab 2 stack 3 stash 4 star 5 start 6 stain 7 stay
8 steal 9 steam 10 steel 11 stem 12 stick 13 stock
14 stop 15 stool 16 stuck 17 stun

1 east 2 best 3 rest 4 test 5 vest 6 west 7 chest
8 fist 9 list 10 cost 11 lost 12 bust 13 dust 14 just 15 must
16 rust 17 beast 18 feast 19 least 20 boast 21 coast 22 roast
23 toast 24 waist

star ☐ stay ☐ steam ☐ stick [1] stop ☐ stool ☐ stun ☐

best ☐ east ☐ list ☐ lost ☐ toast ☐ just ☐ waist ☐

tab		stab		eat		east	
top		stop		vet		vest	
sick		stick		fit		fist	
tool		stool		boat		boast	
seal		steal		wait		waist	
sock		stock		lot		lost	
sack		stack		wet		west	

start   stop   best   east   west

___ ___ ___ ___ ___

1 east 2 ste am 3 stem 4 west 5 coast 6 stock 7 stun 8 must

9 stuck 10 ju st 11 lost 12 stop 13 toast 14 stool 15 least 16 steal 17 waist

18 stay 19 ch e st 20 start 21 bust 22 boast 23 nest 24 quest

the best way	rock star	stop and start
east to west	moon and stars	coast road
The Far East	sun, moon and stars	the east coast
The Far West	see the sun, moon and stars	the west coast

west

east

star   we st   start   east

1 7 a.m. The sun is in the _____ . 3 The car has got a _____ /stop button.
2 7 p.m. The sun is in the _____ . 4 The man is a rock _____ .

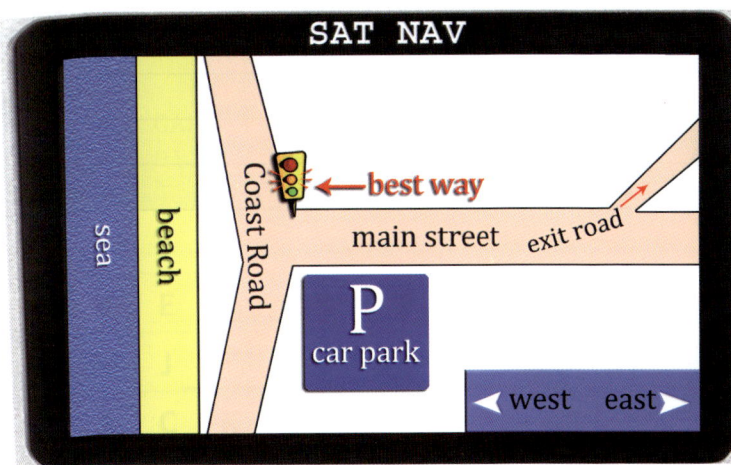

SAT NAV

sea   beach   Coast Road   best way   main street   exit road   P car park   ◄ west   east ►

best	best	BEST	beat
must	must	just	must
start	star	start	start
toast	toast	boast	toast

5 🔊
Read, say and check

6 🔊
Read, then listen and check

7
Complete the sentences with the words in the box

8
Read the words on the sat nav map

9
Find the different word

| B | R | D | R | F | R | G | R | P | R |

1
Read and say

1 **br** 2 **cr** 3 **dr** 4 **fr** 5 **gr**
6 **pr** 7 **tr**

1 **b** 2 **br** 3 **d** 4 **dr** 5 **f** 6 **fr** 7 **g** 8 **gr**
9 **p** 10 **pr**

drum

1 **rain** 2 **brain** 3 **rip** 4 **drip** 5 **rail** 6 **frail**
7 **ram** 8 **gram** 9 **ray** 10 **pray**

1 **bran** 2 **brain** 3 **brash** 4 **breed** 5 **brick** 6 **broom**
7 **brush** 8 **drag** 9 **drain** 10 **dream** 11 **drop** 12 **drip** 13 **drum**

1 **frail** 2 **free** 3 **fresh** 4 **freak** 5 **from** 6 **frost** 7 **grab**
8 **gram** 9 **grand** 10 **green** 11 **greet** 12 **grin** 13 **grip** 14 **grub**
15 **pram** 16 **pray** 17 **prop** 18 **proof** 19 **agree** 20 **afraid**

1 **dream** 2 **cream** 3 **greet** 4 **grand** 5 **fresh** 6 **frost**
7 **pay** 8 **pray** 9 **gram** 10 **gain** 11 **grain** 12 **brush** 13 **brash**
14 **frail** 15 **afraid** 16 **green** 17 **agree** 18 **drain** 19 **brain** 20 **pain**
21 **proof** 22 **grub** 23 **grab** 24 **drum** 25 **frock** 26 **from** 27 **frog**

2
Listen and tick

rain		brain		Pam		pram	
rush		brush		roof		proof	
rip		drip		raid		afraid	
dip		drip		greed		agreed	
fee		free		brain		drain	
frog		frock		bash		brash	
rub		grub		brick		prick	
gain		grain		bran		pram	

3
Trace and write

drag   from   gram   afraid   pray

_____   _____   _____   _____   _____

| B | R | D | R | F | R | G | R | P | R |

FREEWAY: DONT STOP

PAY TODAY AND GET A FREE DVD FROM THIS SHOP

You can pray in this room

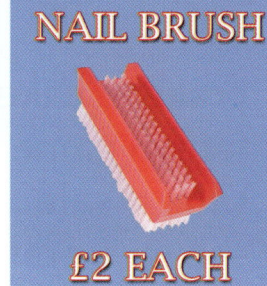

BE GREEN

EGGS FARM FRESH

DANGER! TRAIN TRACK! DO NOT CROSS!

KIDS EAT FREE

NAIL BRUSH
£2 EACH

4
Find and circle the words with *cr* / *br* / *dr* / *fr* / *gr* / *pr* / *tr*

---

pray   free   gram   brain   grand   drop   dream   grab

pram   drain   prop   cream   tray   hand   drab   agree

5
Find words with the same sound

---

say   that   we   you   won't   with

be been each eat he me mean read see seen she _____

bit did him if in this which _____

am an at can had than _____

don't go no so _____

day may _____

do _____

6
Add the key words, then listen and check

---

drag and drop
drumstick
brain drain
brush and broom

free tea
greet me
drop in trash
grab, drag and drop

ten grams
six grams
agree with me
he is afraid

7
Read, then listen and check

---

1 _____   2 _____   3 _____   4 _____   5 _____

8
Dictation

25

A ~ E

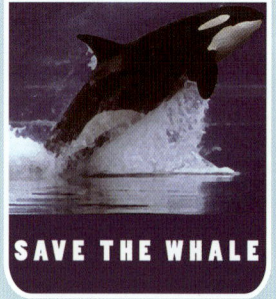

SAVE THE WHALE

1
Read and say

1 **mad**   2 **may**   3 **maid**
4 **made**   5 **Sal**   6 **say**   7 **sail**
8 **sale**

1 **mad**   2 **made**   3 **tap**   4 **tape**
5 **hat**   6 **hate**   7 **can**   8 **cane**   9 **dam**   10 **dame**

1 **brake**   2 **cake**   3 **came**   4 **cane**   5 **case**   6 **dame**   7 **date**
8 **fate**   9 **game**   10 **late**   11 **made**   12 **make**   13 **name**   14 **rave**
15 **safe**   16 **sale**   17 **same**   18 **take**   19 **tape**   20 **wake**   21 **shake**
22 **shave**   23 **state**   24 **brave**   25 **grave**   26 **whale**

1 **came**   2 **same**   3 **fame**   4 **name**   5 **game**   6 **hate**   7 **late**
8 **state**   9 **date**   10 **gate**   11 **mate**   12 **lake**   13 **brake**   14 **cake**
15 **shake**   16 **wake**   17 **brave**   18 **shave**   19 **cave**   20 **grape**
21 **wave**   22 **case**   23 **maze**   24 **tape**   25 **frame**   26 **shape**

2
Listen and tick

bake		brake		fame		frame	
mat		mate		case		base	
gave		grave		late		lane	
can		cane		maze		laze	
Sam		same		safe		sale	
sake		shake		fat		fate	
save		shave		name		mane	

3
Trace and write

made   same   take   date   sale

_____   _____   _____   _____   _____

4
Read and label

grapes   cake   case   gate   date

1 _____   2 _____   3 _____   4 _____   5 _____

5
Tick (✓) the same sounds and cross (✗) the different sounds

fame / farm ☒   cake / brake ☑

1 shame / name ☐   5 bark / bake ☐
2 lack / lake ☐   6 pain / pane ☐
3 ran / rain ☐   7 mate / wait ☐
4 wave / save ☐   8 cash / case ☐

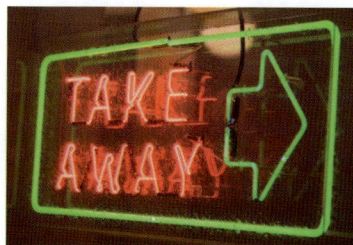

6
Find and circle the words with *ay* / *ay* / *ai*

name: Sam Brain

day: Sunday

date: May 10th

The team will play away this Sunday. It may rain too. Take a coat. Meet me at the gate.

OPTION   SEND

name: Jake Pain

day: Sunday

date: May 10th

We can go on the train and take tea and cake to eat. Don't be late, mate!

OPTION   SEND

7 🔴
Read, say and check

1 sat 2 state 3 cat 4 Kate 5 lack 6 lake 7 shack
8 shake 9 hate 10 hat 11 hay 12 mat 13 may 14 mate
15 greet 16 grate 17 mean 18 save 19 shape 20 fat 21 frame
22 fate 23 name 24 whale

8 🔴
Read, then listen and check

man-made	same day	car brake	bake a cake
late train	farm gate	main name	make tea
wake up	brush shave	same date	shake and wave
brave man	sea wave	Sam came	made from this

9 🔴
Dictation

1 _____ 2 _____ 3 _____ 4 _____ 5 _____

I ~ E

1
Read and say

1 pip 2 pipe 3 dim 4 dime
5 lick 6 like 7 fin 8 fine
9 quit 10 quite

pipeline

1 Sid 2 side 3 Tim 4 time
5 sit 6 site + 7 I 8 I'm

1 bike 2 chime 3 crime 4 dine 5 file 6 fine 7 five
8 life 9 like 10 lime 11 line 12 mile 13 mine 14 nine
15 ride 16 side 17 tide 18 time 19 wide 20 wife 21 shine
22 drive 23 bride 24 tribe 25 while 26 white 27 I'm

1 ride 2 mine 3 hike 4 quite 5 like 6 while 7 fine
8 white 9 five 10 bribe 11 nine 12 shine 13 drive 14 wife
15 crime 16 life 17 time 18 file 19 I'm 20 chime 21 wide
22 pipe 23 line 24 pipeline

3 three   5 five   7 seven   9 nine   10 ten

2
Listen and tick

mad		made		sit		site	
can		cane		bit		bite	
hat		hate		wit		white	
pip		pipe		rat		rate	
Tim		time		dim		dime	
quit		quite		dam		dame	
lick		like		Lin		line	

3
Trace and write

I   I'm   like   life   fine

_____ _____ _____ _____ _____

mine   time   while   quite

_____ _____ _____ _____

Has it got ___ sides?

It is a can of ___-up.

It has ___ stars.

It is Exit ___ B.

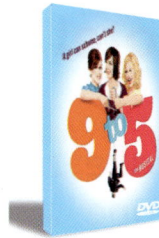

It is a DVD of ___ To Five.

4
Complete the sentences

---

bid / bride	☒	bike / like	☑

1 shin / shine ☐	**4** pin / pine ☐	**7** life / wife ☐	**10** shin / sin ☐
2 fin / sin ☐	**5** him / time ☐	**8** pick / pike ☐	**11** Rick / bike ☐
3 crime / chime ☐	**6** bride / wide ☐	**9** rip / ripe ☐	**12** lime / I'm ☐

5
Tick (✓) the same sounds and cross (✗) the different sounds

Mick   Mike   Jack   Jake   Nick   Sam   James   Jim   Jo   Jeff
Jan   Jane   Tom   Tim   Kate   Nat   Jade   Dan   Stan   Rick
Miles   Niles

6
Read the names

Hi, I'm Kate.
I'm from China

Hi, I'm Jake.
I'm from Canada

7
Read the sentences

Hi, I'm Jan. / Hi, I'm Jane.
I'm not from China.

Hi, I'm Mick. / Hi, I'm Mike.
I'm not from Canada.

8
Read, then listen and check

---

lifeline	I like Mike	Is it mine?
pipeline	We like Jane	Is it on time?
five bikes	I don't like Nick	Is it Mike?
a wide lake	Mike likes him	Am I from China?

---

1 _____ **2** _____ **3** _____ **4** _____ **5** _____

9
Dictation

27 O ~ E

1 **not** 2 **note** 3 **cod** 4 **code**
5 **hop** 6 **hope** 7 **rob** 8 **robe**
9 **pop** 10 **pope**

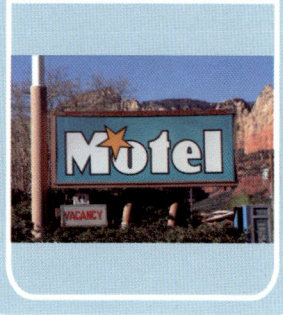

1 **hot** 2 **hotel** 3 **hoe** 4 **boat**

1 bone 2 broke 3 code 4 cone 5 cope 6 cove 7 drove
8 home 9 hope 10 joke 11 lone 12 rode 13 rope 14 tone
15 vote 16 woke 17 probe 18 stone 19 stove 20 zone

1 motel 2 hotel 3 vote 4 note 5 bone 6 cone 7 lone
8 tone 9 stone 10 home 11 broke 12 joke 13 woke 14 cove
15 zone 16 hope 17 rope 18 drove 19 stove 20 probe

1 rod 2 rode 3 red 4 read 5 home 6 hot 7 broke
8 motel 9 wick 10 woke 11 wake 12 weak 13 zone 14 lone
15 loan 16 loon 17 noon 18 rope 19 probe 20 rob 21 robe
22 bone

not		note		home		hope	
wok		woke		stone		stove	
Jock		joke		probe		robe	
mod		mode		rope		robe	
lob		lobe		bone		tone	
cod		code		lone		zone	
hop		hope		rode		rope	

steel   wood   stone   brick   rope

It's made of ___ | It's made of ___ | It's made of ___ | It's made of ___ | It's made of ___

4
Read, then listen and check

5
Number the words, then listen and check

6
Read, then listen and check

7
Dictation

The Texas West Hotel Dallas: time zones

Dallas	Rome	China	Japan
Dall • as	Rome	Chi • na	Jap • an

1 = *o* in *hot*   **2** = *oo* in *zoo*   **3** = *o* in *coat, no, foe, vote*

vote	**3**	hot	**1**	zoo	**2**
Rome		shoot		rope	
roof		foam		so	
coach		moon		sock	
soon		stove		food	
joke		toe		probe	
go		hotel		goat	
hope		got		not	
lock		note		motel	

The New Forest

40 ZONE

time zone
a hotel in Rome
a stone road
a hot stove
the green zone

he woke up
she drove home
a safe zone
ride a bike
he broke a bone

he is late home
don't park in this zone
don't stop in that zone
don't go home late
we won't be late

1 _____ **2** _____ **3** _____ **4** _____ **5** _____

28

| A | B | C | D | E |

1 see   B C D E G P T V

2 get   F L M N S X Z

3 day   A H J K

4 you   Q U W

5 hi   I Y

6 go   O

7 car   R

The names of the letters

A B C D E F G H I J K L M N O P Q R S T U V W X Y Z

2
Put the letters
A–Z in the boxes
with the same
vowel sound

do	make	mean	men	so	park	pipe
	A					

A B C D E F G H I J K L M N O P Q R S T U V W X Y Z

1 _____ **2** _____ **3** _____ **4** _____ **5** _____

6 _____ **7** _____ **8** _____ **9** _____ **10** _____

1 wipe **2** time **3** Friday **4** Hi **5** I **6** hi-fi **7** pi

CD	DNA	OK	USA	BMW	www
http	UN	CNN	ABC	TDK	EU
CBS	MTV	L.A.	DVD-RW	VW	USB
iPod	eBay	a.m.	p.m.		

bbc.co.uk BBC home ☐

CNN.com ☐

⬧TDK ☐

 iPod ☐

USB ☐

 ☐

eBay – New & used electronics, cars, apparel, collectibles, sporting goods & more at low prices

http://www.ebay.com/

Bookmarks	news	web	websites
Time:	> BBC	> eBay	> www.tom.jones.net.au
09:30 a.m.	> CNN	> iPod	> www.bmw.com.de
Friday 4 May	> CBS	> Google	> www.see.tv.com
	> NBC	> Yahoo!	> www.dvd.uk.com
	> LA Times	> hotmail	> www.OK.mag.com

B L C L F L

1 **bl** 2 **cl** 3 **fl** 4 **gl** 5 **pl** 6 **sl**

1 **b** 2 **br** 3 **bl** 4 **c** 5 **cr** 6 **cl** 7 **f** 8 **fr**
9 **fl** 10 **p** 11 **pr** 12 **pl** 13 **s** 14 **sl**

1 **back** 2 **black** 3 **cub** 4 **club** 5 **fat** 6 **flat**
7 **gum** 8 **glum** 9 **pan** 10 **plan** 11 **seep** 12 **sleep**

1 **bleed** 2 **block** 3 **bloom** 4 **blush** 5 **clap** 6 **clean** 7 **clock**
8 **flash** 9 **flea** 10 **float** 11 **glad** 12 **glen** 13 **gloom** 14 **plane**
15 **play** 16 **please** 17 **slap** 18 **slot** 19 **slope** 20 **slum**

1 **flea** 2 **sleep** 3 **clean** 4 **please** 5 **bleed** 6 **blush** 7 **club**
8 **clock** 9 **block** 10 **slot** 11 **gloom** 12 **bloom** 13 **float** 14 **slope**
15 **slap** 16 **clap** 17 **flat** 18 **glad** 19 **black** 20 **flash** 21 **plan** 22 **play**
23 **plane** 24 **glen** 25 **slum**

back		black		lad		glad	
lack		black		pea		plea	
cap		clap		pay		play	
lap		clap		pray		play	
lean		clean		sheep		sleep	
beach		bleach		lot		slot	
lash		flash		sum		slum	
flock		frock		cram		clam	

clock   please   play   sleep

_____   _____   _____   _____

USB flash drive   alarm clock   float plane   black and green

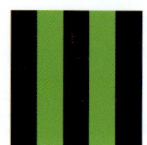

1 _____   2 _____   3 _____   4 _____

5
Find the different word

6
Find the words

7
Read, then listen and check

8
Read the key words

9
Read, say and check

play	*play*	pray	**play**	play
please	please	please	*please*	**plead**
clock	clock	*crock*	clock	clock
plane	**plate**	PLANE	*plane*	*plane*

remote control

on/off sleep TV
VHS DVD HDD
1 2 3
4 5 6
7 8 9
-/- 0 home
BACK PLAY STOP
CHECK TIME SET TIME NEXT PROG
VOL REC CHANNEL

play	sleep
home	TV
HDD	DVD
stop	on
check time	off

1 clock 2 flock 3 lot 4 plot 5 flat 6 flash 7 boom 8 bloom
9 free 10 flea 11 pray 12 play 13 pea 14 plea 15 please

OK please I won't you and do don't Hi while

yes, please	please wait	glad to meet you
please stay	play an MP3	go to sleep
tea, please	USB flash drive	planes, boats and trains
coffee, please	a black flash drive	please clean this

Blu-ray Disc™

mp3™

DVD VIDEO™

61

~ N D ~ N K

1 nd **2** nk **3** nt **4** nch

1 a**nd** **2** i**nk** **3** a**nt** **4** i**nch**

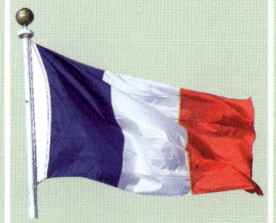

French flag

1 band **2** hand **3** land **4** blend **5** stand
6 gland **7** grand **8** end **9** fond **10** pond **11** bank **12** tank
13 drink **14** link **15** pink **16** junk **17** went **18** sent **19** don't
20 print **21** grunt **22** French **23** bunch **24** lunch **25** quench

1 land **2** lend **3** link **4** lunch **5** band **6** bend **7** bank
8 French **9** bunch **10** drink **11** drank **12** drunk **13** grunt
14 grand **15** end **16** gland **17** junk **18** quench **19** crunch
20 went **21** sent **22** pink **23** pinch **24** wink **25** bond

1 sink **2** paint **3** blond **4** bland **5** blend **6** trench **7** plank
8 prank **9** chunk **10** trunk **11** flinch **12** blink **13** crank **14** punk
15 punch **16** clink **17** brand **18** bench **19** faint **20** mint **21** hint
22 winch

and		ant		French		quench	
in		ink		crush		crunch	
hand		Hank		bun		bunch	
band		bank		went		wench	
drink		drank		link		drink	
ink		inch		end		and	
pink		pinch		pond		bond	

end   and   went   lunch   drink

____ ____ ____ ____ ____

hand   ant   ink   drink   bunch of grapes

1 _____ 2 _____ 3 _____ 4 _____ 5 _____

end	*and*	end	end	END
lunch	lunch	*lunch*	bunch	LUNCH
DRINK	drunk	**drink**	*drink*	**drink**
went	**went**	want	**went**	*went*

🌐 website   📧 inbox   ✉ e-mail   🖨 print   ⏲ time 2:30 p.m.   ⓘ date 8 May

paint program

tools	
⬚ crop	A a font
🖊 pen	brush
paint pot	🌲 clip art
╲ line	〰 free line
☐○▲ shapes	🗑 trash
red	green

white   black   blue   pink

a grandstand
Land's End
stop junk mail
send junk mail

a weblink
a pink drink
a black tank
a French bank

eat and drink
eat lunch
end lunch
lunchtime

punch drunk
a punk band
a mint drink
a French man

1 _____   2 _____   3 _____

4 _____   5 _____   6 _____

~ N G

King Kong

1 Read and say

1 ing   2 ang   3 ong   4 ung

1 win   2 wi**ng**   3 ban   4 ba**ng**
5 lon   6 lo**ng**   7 run   8 ru**ng**

1 king   2 ring   3 sing   4 wing   5 bring   6 cling   7 fling
8 sling   9 sting   10 swing   11 bang   12 hang   13 rang   14 sang
15 slang   16 long   17 song   18 rung   19 stung   20 swung

1 sing   2 singing   3 ring   4 ringing   5 bring   6 bringing
7 bang   8 banging   9 drink   10 drinking   11 eat   12 eating   13 go
14 going   15 do   16 doing   17 speak   18 speaking   19 read
20 reading   21 play   22 playing   23 say   24 saying

2 Listen and tick

ban		bang		ring		ringing	
sin		sing		ringing		bringing	
ran		rang		paying		playing	
kin		king		eating		meeting	
stun		stung		reading		feeding	
hand		hang		singing		swinging	
clean		cling		hanging		banging	

3 Trace and write

ring   ringing   long   saying

_____   _____   _____   _____

4 Complete the sentences

eating   singing   reading   sleeping   drinking

He is   She is   He is   He is   She is

1 _____   2 _____   3 _____   4 _____   5 _____

5
Circle the CAPITAL letters

6
Label the flags

7
Read, then listen and check

8
Dictation

English   Beijing   China   Bangkok   British   Hong Kong   Bangladesh

French   Dutch   English   British   Swiss

1 _____ 2 _____ 3 _____ 4 _____ 5 _____

1 English (ing-lish) 2 Beijing (bay-jing) 3 Shanghai (shang-hi)
4 Hong Kong 5 Bangladesh 6 Bangkok 7 British

1 A British plane 2 A Swiss bank 3 A Greek flag 4 A Dutch car
5 An English man 6 A French boat

1 _____   2 _____   3 _____

4 _____

| O | R | O | R | E | A | W |

1
Read and say

1 o **2** oo **3** oa **4** or **5** ore
6 oor **7** aw

1 or **2** for **3** more **4** door
5 saw **+** **6** your **7** four

1 born **2** fork **3** morning **4** short **5** sort **6** sport **7** storm
8 torch **9** core **10** chore **11** score **12** store **13** swore **14** poor
15 moor **16** floor **17** four **18** your **19** law **20** jaw **21** saw **22** draw
23 dawn **24** prawn **25** lawn

1 more **2** moor **3** morning **4** saw **5** swore **6** storm **7** law
8 lawn **9** born **10** drawn **11** prawn **12** jaw **13** your **14** for
15 four **16** floor **17** torch **18** chore **19** Ford

2
Number from
1–7

four [1]   fork [ ]   score [ ]   jaw [ ]   chore [ ]   store [ ]   your [ ]

poor [ ]   born [ ]   sport [ ]   spot [ ]   short [ ]   sort [ ]   shot [ ]

3
Listen and tick

sport		sort		shore		short	
pot		port		short		shot	
law		lawn		prawn		poor	
fork		four		core		chore	
your		jaw		draw		door	
spot		sport		saw		store	
floor		for		or		er	

4
Trace and write

for   born   more   morning   saw

_____ _____ _____ _____ _____

fork

score

door

four

torch

5
Read and label

1 _____ **2** _____ **3** _____ **4** _____ **5** _____

6
Match the same words

law	your
prawn	*saw*
lawn	four
saw	LAW
four	*prawn*
your	lawn

door	born
born	**sport**
poor	short
more	door
sport	MORE
SHORT	*poor*

7
Find words from Unit 33

N	F	L	O	O	R	J	H
M	O	R	N	I	N	G	X
B	U	J	Q	M	O	R	E
D	R	A	W	L	R	S	Y
Z	P	W	X	A	T	A	O
B	O	R	N	W	H	W	U
M	O	S	C	O	R	E	R
P	R	A	W	N	P	A	W

THE ALL NEW FORD FOCUS 4-DOOR ST

A four-door Ford car

8 🔴
Read, then listen and check

4	14	15	16	17	19
four	fourteen	fifteen	sixteen	seventeen	nineteen

■ car / a Ford car / four doors / a four-door car / a four-door Ford car
■ your car / your four-door car / a sports car / a four-door sports car
■ born / born at dawn / born in the morning / I was born in May.
■ sweetcorn / eat sweetcorn / prawns / sweetcorn and prawns
■ a storm / rain and storm / law / court / a law court / in a law court

9 🔴
Dictation

1 _____

2 _____

O W O U

OUT

1 o 2 or 3 ore 4 ow 5 ou

1 **now** 2 **how** 3 **out** 4 **about** 5 **loud** 6 **sound**

1 **how** 2 **now** 3 **cow** 4 **vow** 5 **Wow!** 6 **down** 7 **gown** 8 **town** 9 **brown** 10 **clown** 11 **crowd** 12 **crown** 13 **drown** 14 **out** 15 **shout** 16 **loud** 17 **cloud** 18 **proud** 19 **found** 20 **round** 21 **sound** 22 **ground** 23 **count** 24 **pound** 25 **about**

1 **out** 2 **now** 3 **drown** 4 **count** 5 **ground** 6 **town** 7 **cloud** 8 **brown** 9 **vow** 10 **shout** 11 **cow** 12 **drown** 13 **pound** 14 **gown** 15 **sound** 16 **down** 17 **round** 18 **crown** 19 **crowd** 20 **loud** 21 **cloud** 22 **found** 23 **Wow!** 24 **about** 25 **how**

1 **mount** 2 **hound** 3 **noun** 4 **snout** 5 **shouting** 6 **counting** 7 **drowning** 8 **prow** 9 **crowding** 10 **rounding**

no ☐ nor ☐ now ☐ out ☐1 round ☐ proud ☐ down ☐

now		Ow!		round		ground	
town		down		noun		now	
brown		drown		loud		cloud	
clown		crown		out		Ow!	
crowd		cloud		how		cow	
proud		pound		sound		pound	
vow		Wow!		loud		proud	

out   now   how   round   town

___   ___   ___   ___   ___

brown cow   down   pound   cloud   crowd

   £

1 _____ 2 _____ 3 _____ 4 _____ 5 _____

now	now	*noun*	now	*now*
how?	how?	How?	*now?*	*how?*
about	about	around	*about*	*about*
out	our	*out*	out	out

a • bout   about
round • a • bout   roundabout
mount • ain   mountain
fount • ain   fountain
down • town   downtown
morn • ing   morning
es • cape   escape
Eng • lish   English
four • teen   fourteen
sev • en • teen   seventeen
ho • tel   hotel
rail • way   railway
pro • gram   program

roundabout

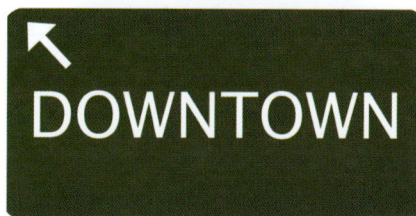
DOWNTOWN

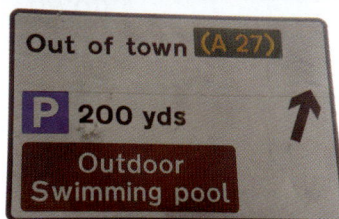
Out of town (A 27)
P 200 yds
Outdoor Swimming pool

a downtown car park
a dark brown cow
about ten o'clock
shout out loud
a loud sound

a mountain railway
down a mountain
a book about the town
go round and round
fourteen pounds

a town fountain
a big roundabout
look around the town
a ground-floor flat
I found a pound

5
Read and label

6
Find the different word

7
Read, say and check

8
Read, then listen and check

35

1
Read and say

1 I 2 Hi 3 **by** 4 **my** 5 **why**
+ 6 **buy** 7 **guy**

fly

1 E 2 fun 3 **funny** 4 dad
5 **daddy** 6 wind 7 **windy**

1 **by** 2 **cry** 3 **dry** 4 **fly** 5 **fry** 6 **ply** 7 **pry** 8 **my** 9 **sky**
10 **sly** 11 **spy** 12 **try** 13 **why** 14 **buy** 15 **guy** 16 **byte** 17 **megabyte**
18 **Wi-Fi** 19 **hi-fi**

1 **happy** 2 **lobby** 3 **lorry** 4 **jetty** 5 **funny** 6 **mummy**
7 **daddy** 8 **nanny** 9 **choppy** 10 **grubby** 11 **sunny** 12 **windy**
13 **cloudy** 14 **rainy** 15 **silly** 16 **angry** 17 **hungry**

1 **happy** 2 **daddy** 3 **windy** 4 **silly** 5 **rainy** 6 **cloudy** 7 **choppy**
8 **sunny** 9 **my** 10 **try** 11 **fry** 12 **cry** 13 **byte** 14 **sky** 15 **fly** 16 **sly**
17 **guy** 18 **dry** 19 **by** 20 **why** 21 **guy** 22 **angry** 23 **hungry** 24 **buy**

1 **dying** 2 **drying** 3 **crying** 4 **flying** 5 **frying** 6 **lying**
7 **spying** 8 **trying** 9 **buying**

2
Listen and tick

my		by		lobby		lorry	
sky		spy		happy		hippy	
by		byte		funny		sunny	
fly		fry		angry		hungry	
ply		pry		jetty		Getty	
cry		try		daddy		Danny	
why		Hi		hi-fi		Wi-Fi	

3
Trace and write

my   by   why   happy   guy

___ ___ ___ ___ ___

ply / play	☒	why / while	☑
1 shy / shine	☐	**5** my / mine	☐
2 buy / by	☐	**6** my / may	☐
3 bit / byte	☐	**7** sly / slay	☐
4 try / tree	☐	**8** cry / crime	☐

HOT SPOT
FREE
Wi Fi
ZONE

4
Tick (✓) the same sounds and cross (✗) the different sounds

Shanghai

hot ☐ dry ☐ sunny ☐ wet ☐ rain ☐ foggy ☐ cloudy ☐
windy ☐ storms ☐

5 🔊
Listen to the weather reports for Shanghai and Tokyo and tick (✓) the words you hear

Tokyo

hot ☐ dry ☐ sunny ☐ wet ☐ rain ☐ foggy ☐ cloudy ☐
windy ☐ storms ☐

him say down why or been go mean the

a about am an and & at @ be _____ bit born but by can count day
did do doing don't _____ drink each eat English for from get _____
going got had he Hi _____ how if I in it just let lot may me _____
morning much must my no not now OK on _____ out please pound read
room saw _____ see seen she shop so soon than that _____ them this
too up us we went when which while _____ with won't yes you your

6 🔊
Add the key words, then listen and check

⊕ website   ✉ inbox   ✉ e-mail   🖨 print   ⏱ time15.30   ⓘ date 14 May   📶 Wi-Fi

Hong Kong
dry, sunny
22°C

Dallas
hot, sunny,
blue sky
30°C

Rome
wet, raining
16°C

Beijing
cloudy sky
27°C

Paris
dark, foggy
9°C

Bangkok
storm, windy
17°C

7
Find and circle words from Unit 35

36

O Y ~ O I ~

toy lorry

1 Read and say

1 o 2 oo 3 oa 4 or 5 ow
6 oy 7 oi

1 boy 2 toy 3 oil 4 coin

1 boy 2 coy 3 joy 4 soy 5 soya 6 toy 7 loyal 8 royal 9 enjoy 10 employ 11 annoy 12 oil 13 boil 14 coil 15 coin 16 foil 17 join 18 joint 19 loin 20 soil 21 toil 22 avoid 23 point 24 spoil

1 boy 2 boil 3 coy 4 coil 5 joy 6 join 7 enjoy 8 soy 9 soil 10 soya 11 toil 12 toy 13 coin 14 point 15 oil 16 spoil 17 joint 18 avoid 19 annoy 20 employ 21 foil 22 royal 23 loyal 24 loin

1 soya 2 point 3 pointing 4 annoy 5 annoying 6 avoid 7 avoiding 8 coin 9 coy 10 oil 11 boil 12 join 13 joint 14 joy 15 enjoy 16 soy 17 day 18 by 19 fly 20 flay 21 toy 22 toil 23 soil 24 spoil 25 boiling 26 joining 27 enjoying

2 Number from 1–7

oil ☐ soil 1 soy ☐ employ ☐ avoid ☐ point ☐ annoy ☐

3 Listen and tick

toy		toil		point		appoint	
soil		spoil		void		avoid	
boy		boil		joy		enjoy	
joy		join		oil		royal	
join		joint		loyal		royal	
soy		soil		loin		join	
coy		coin		soy		soya	

4 Trace and write

oil ____ boy ____ enjoy ____ point ____

coins

1 = o in *hot*   2 = oi/oy in *boy*   3 = o in *coat, no, foe, vote*   4 = or in *born*

soap	**3**	lot	**1**	toy	**2**	born	**4**
drawn		point		don't		woke	
hotel		cord		job		spoil	
rope		boil		joy		fond	
boy		song		bone		more	
joint		poor		torch		hope	
swore		soil		stove		prawn	
annoy		snob		floor		spot	
long		got		avoid		coin	

a pound coin
a round coin
four-megabyte
soya bean

boil sweetcorn
point at the floor
bones and joints
boiling oil

coins and cards
a boy and a toy
soil and toil
enjoy your lunch

1 _____ **2** _____ **3** _____ **4** _____ **5** _____

WAIT TIME
APPROX
15
MINS
FROM THIS POINT

cashpoint

TOYS (25)

TOYMASTER

No Eating
Beyond This Point

API SERVICE SLICE
SAE
10W-30
ACEA A3/B
A3/B4-04
API SL/CP

SAE 10W-30
MOTOR OIL

Royal Mail

Coins & Cards

5
Number the
words, then listen
and check

6
Read, then listen
and check

7
Dictation

8
Find words with
oi / oy

37

I R U R O R

[1] ar [2] or [3] oy [4] ir [5] ur
+ [6] her [7] word

[1] sir [2] bird [3] first [4] fur [5] surf
[6] her [7] world

bird

[1] bird [2] first [3] girl [4] sir [5] fur [6] flirt [7] skirt [8] shirt
[9] stir [10] swirl [11] her [12] burn [13] church [14] curl [15] burst [16] blur
[17] lurk [18] surf [19] spur [20] turn [21] Turk [22] word [23] work [24] worst
[25] worm [26] world [27] herb

[1] fur [2] first [3] turn [4] surf [5] spur [6] burn [7] blur [8] burst
[9] worst [10] bird [11] word [12] her [13] girl [14] curl [15] Turk [16] lurk
[17] work [18] flirt [19] shirt [20] sir [21] skirt [22] herb [23] church
[24] swirl

sir ☐ first ☐ girl [1] turn ☐ work ☐ word ☐ her ☐

shirt		skirt		fist		first	
word		work		bad		bird	
burn		turn		for		fur	
fur		first		shot		shirt	
sir		surf		ward		word	
lurk		Turk		warm		worm	
spur		stir		Carl		curl	

first   her   word   girl   turn

_____   _____   _____   _____   _____

boy and girl

5
Complete the sentences

6
Read and copy

7 🏀
Read, say and check

8 🏀
Read, then listen and check

| surfing | laptop | world | looking | mug |

1. He has got a black _____.
2. He has got a _____ of coffee.
3. He is _____ the net.
4. He is _____ at a website.
5. The Internet is the '_____ wide web'.

WORLD HOTEL

Dry cleaning list

shirt		coat	
skirt		waistcoat	
pants		T-shirt	
frock / dress		top	

Please tick the items.
Place the list in a bag.

Name	Jenny Burns
Date	1st May
Room	14 (fourteen)

shirts

pink top

W___LD HOTEL

Dry cl___ning list

shirt		c___t	
sk___t		w___stc___t	
pants		T-sh___t	
frock / dress		top	

Pl___se tick the items.
Place the list in a bag.

Name	Jenny Burns
Date	1st May
R____m	14 (fourteen)

---

1. for 2. fur 3. far 4. tar 5. tore 6. Turk 7. burn 8. born 9. world 10. Hamburg
11. wore 12. whirl 13. girl 14. word 15. church 16. surf 17. surfing 18. turf 19. first
20. turban 21. turning 22. her 23. herb 24. burning 25. working 26. turning
27. lurk 28. fork

1st = first   @ = at   & = and   £ = pounds   + = plus

www = World Wide Web   .com = dot com

&   .com   +   1st   @   £   www

---

surf the net	boy and girl	her skirt	yes, sir
world wide web	English words	his shirt	no, sir
turn up	Turkish coffee	my fur coat	please, sir
turn down	Word program	your sock	go first, sir

38

~ C E C E ~ C I ~

1 **ace** 2 **ice** 3 **face** 4 **nice**
5 **peace** 6 **voice**

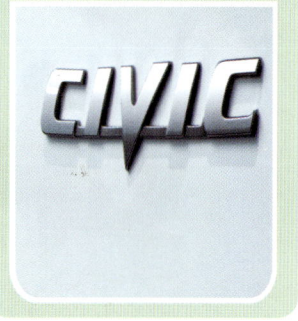

CIVIC

1 **cent** 2 **her** 3 **cert** 4 **circus**
5 **cite** 6 **civic**

1 ace 2 face 3 pace 4 place 5 race 6 space 7 trace
8 ice 9 dice 10 mice 11 nice 12 price 13 rice 14 slice
15 spice 16 twice 17 vice 18 plaice 19 force 20 fleece
21 peace 22 voice 23 choice 24 ice cream

1 cent 2 central 3 centi 4 centigram 5 centigrade
6 cement 7 cert 8 certain 9 cite 10 civic 11 civil 12 circus
13 citrus 14 cinema

pace		place		cite		kite	
space		spice		cent		Kent	
ice		rice		mice		Mike	
face		force		face		fake	
vice		voice		spice		spike	
nice		mice		race		rake	
ace		face		force		fork	

nice   cent   peace   voice   cinema

_____ _____ _____ _____ _____

centigrade   centimetre   centigrams   centipede   century

1701–1800
1801–1900
1901-2000

1 _____ 2 _____ 3 _____ 4 _____ 5 _____

5
Find the new words and circle them

	Japan	rice, soyabeans, fish, seafood, seaweed
	China	rice, wheat, beans, pork
	USA	wheat, corn (maize), rice, beef, pork, chicken, turkey, milk
	UK	wheat, oats, chicken, lamb, pork, beef, milk, eggs, cheese

cent • i • grade
cent • i • gram
cy • cling   cy = sy   cl = kl
cir • cus   cir = sir   cus = kus
cer • tain   cir = sir

6
Read, then listen and check

a nice ice cream
no cycling
ten centigrade
ten cents each
yes, it's certain
four grams of rice
the space race
a French circus
the marketplace

MOSCOW STATE CIRCUS

P 60 Spaces

NO CYCLING
st Dorset District Counc

ICE CREAM

Nice Price!

MARKET PLACE

7
Read, say and check

1 ___ 2 ___ 3 ___ 4 ___ 5 ___

8
Dictation

39

~ E R

1 **big** 2 **bigger** 3 **hot** 4 **hotter**
5 **win** 6 **winner**

letter

1 **pep** 2 **pepper** 3 **rub**
4 **rubber** 5 **fat** 6 **fatter** 7 **sing**
8 **singer** 9 **bank** 10 **banker**

1 **better** 2 **letter** 3 **pepper** 4 **hammer** 5 **spammer**
6 **manner** 7 **matter** 8 **planner** 9 **shower** 10 **rubber**
11 **butter** 12 **hotter** 13 **copper** 14 **bigger** 15 **burger**
16 **winner** 17 **tipper** 18 **singer** 19 **heater** 20 **worker** 21 **waiter**

1 **butter** 2 **better** 3 **banker** 4 **spammer** 5 **shower**
6 **planner** 7 **manner** 8 **winner** 9 **singer** 10 **pepper**
11 **copper** 12 **tipper** 13 **burger** 14 **bigger** 15 **letter** 16 **worker**
17 **hotter** 18 **waiter** 19 **hammer** 20 **rubber** 21 **matter**

1 **sleeper** 2 **litter** 3 **waiter** 4 **speaker** 5 **toaster**
6 **swimmer** 7 **steamer** 8 **trainer** 9 **sneaker** 10 **browser**
11 **farmer** 12 **boiler** 13 **border** 14 **pointer** 15 **scanner**
16 **printer** 17 **power** 18 **order**

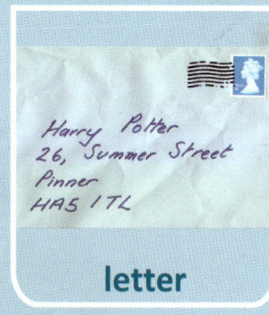

win	winner	better	butter
work	worker	letter	litter
sing	singer	bigger	burger
plan	planner	hotter	heater
rub	rubber	spammer	hammer
pepper	tipper	letter	better
manner	matter	better	pepper

better   pepper   worker   bigger

_____   _____   _____   _____

4
Read and label

butter

beefburger

red pepper

black pepper

| 1 _____ | 2 _____ | 3 _____ | 4 _____ |

printer

hammer

scanner

speaker

| 5 _____ | 6 _____ | 7 _____ | 8 _____ |

5
Find and circle words from Unit 39

Try a bigger, better burger here today (100% beef)

bur • ger   burger   pep • per   pepper
prin • ter   printer   wait • er   waiter
swim • mer   swimmer   toast • er   toaster

6
Read, say and check

a copper hammer   toast and butter   send me a letter
a power shower   more pepper, please   a web browser
printer and scanner a shower of rain   a bigger beefburger

7
Read, then listen and check

| E | E | R | E | A | R | E | R | E |

1 Read and say

1 **ar**   2 **ir**   3 **ur**   4 **er**   5 **eer**
6 **ear**   7 **ere**

PAY HERE FOR SHORT STAY ONLY

1 **deer**   2 **cheer**   3 **ear**   4 **near**
5 **here**   6 **we're**

1 **deer** 2 **peer** 3 **cheer** 4 **jeer** 5 **queer** 6 **sneer** 7 **dear**
8 **fear** 9 **gear** 10 **hear** 11 **near** 12 **rear** 13 **tear** 14 **year**
15 **beard** 16 **clear** 17 **spear** 18 **here** 19 **we're** 20 **earring**
21 **hearing**

1 **deer** 2 **dear** 3 **hear** 4 **here** 5 **gear** 6 **jeer** 7 **year**
8 **near** 9 **we're** 10 **clear** 11 **cheer** 12 **queer** 13 **sneer** 14 **beard**
15 **peer** 16 **tear** 17 **rear** 18 **ear** 19 **spear** 20 **hearing** 21 **fear**

2 Number from 1–7

we're ☐   here ☐   fear ☐   year 1   near ☐   dear ☐   cheer ☐

3 Listen and tick

rear		clear		far		fear	
cheer		clear		spur		spear	
sneer		spear		beard		board	
jeer		year		poor		peer	
queer		clear		tar		tear	
gear		jeer		fear		fur	
earring		hearing		your		year	

4 Trace and write

near   here   we're   year   cheer

5 Read and label

gear   spear   beard   deer   ear

1 _____   2 _____   3 _____   4 _____   5 _____

1 far 2 fear 3 fur 4 fame 5 here 6 her 7 hark 8 get 9 grade 10 gear 11 jar 12 jeer 13 dear 14 date 15 queen 16 queer 17 clench 18 clear 19 yard 20 yet 21 year 22 your 23 store 24 stir 25 steer 26 star 27 beard 28 bard 29 word

TopGear

ORDER HERE

cheer up

1 = *ear* in *near*   2 = *ir* in *first*   3 = *ar* in *park*   4 = *or* in *born*

farm	3	gear	1	burn	2	lawn	4
flirt		hard		year		bird	
worst		jaw		bark		cheer	
fork		her		surf		skirt	
near		here		queer		start	
far		harp		sir		floor	
fear		chart		store		dear	
four		shirt		rear		world	
girl		clear		card		we're	

it's near here
we hear it's near
We're here!
I can hear her

steer clear
cheer, don't jeer
cheering and booing
please pay here

top gear
stop here
don't stop here
a brown beard

PAY & DISPLAY
CAR PARK
PAY HERE

6 🔊
Read, then listen and check

7 🔊
Number the words, then listen and check

8 🔊
Read, then listen and check

A I R ~ A R E

Airport ✈

1 Read and say

1 a 2 ai 3 ar 4 ear 5 er
6 ur 7 air 8 are

1 **air** 2 p**air** 3 c**are** 4 squ**are**

1 air 2 fair 3 hair 4 chair 5 stair 6 dairy 7 fairy 8 hairy
9 airport 10 bare 11 care 12 dare 13 fare 14 hare 15 mare
16 rare 17 flare 18 glare 19 scare 20 square 21 share 22 spare

1 fair 2 mare 3 hare 4 hair 5 hairy 6 chair 7 share
8 flare 9 fairy 10 dare 11 dairy 12 air 13 fare 14 airfare
15 airport 16 bare 17 care 18 scare 19 square 20 stair 21 glare

2 Number from 1–7

air ☐ fair ☐ hair ☐ square ☐ dare ☐ rare [1] glare ☐

3 Listen and tick

far		fair	
car		care	
pain		pair	
her		hair	
bar		bare	
flame		flare	
stain		stair	

dare		dairy	
fair		fairy	
spare		square	
glaze		glare	
shave		share	
chain		chair	
scar		scare	

4 Trace and write

air   hair   pair   share   square

___   ___   ___   ___   ___

5 Read and label

brown hair   stairs   chair   square   armchair

  ☐

1 _____ 2 _____ 3 _____ 4 _____ 5 _____

air　　airlines　　airways　　aero　　Swissair　　British　　American

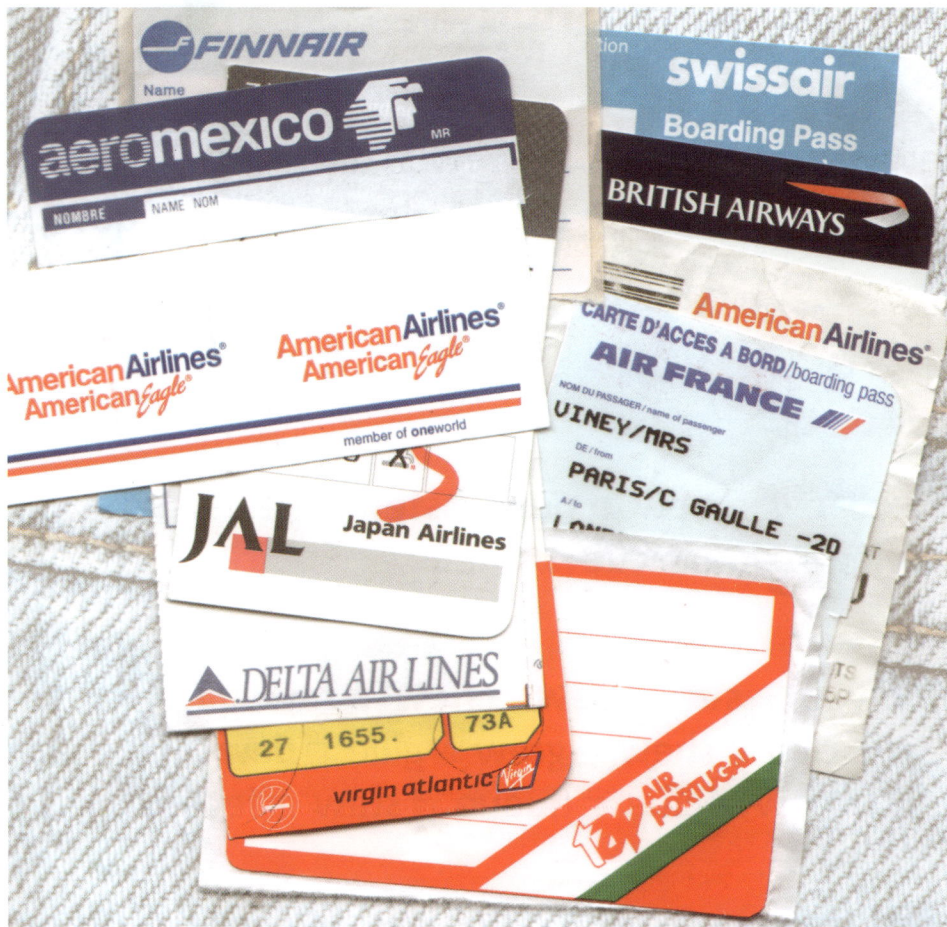

6
Find and circle the words

1 fur　**2** fear　**3** far　**4** fair　**5** four　**6** airfare　**7** ferry　**8** fairy　**9** star　**10** stir　**11** stair　**12** stare　**13** bore　**14** bar　**15** bare　**16** bird　**17** scar　**18** skirt　**19** scare　**20** her　**21** hair　**22** hungry　**23** hairy　**24** round　**25** square　**26** part　**27** port　**28** pair

a dairy farm	airfare	it's not fair
pairwork	rail fare	that's my chair
a square box	bus fare	it's not a spare chair

1 _____ **2** _____ **3** _____ **4** _____

7
Read, say and check

8
Read, then listen and check

9
Dictation

← **STAIRS**

E W U E

1 o 2 oo 3 too 4 crew 5 flew
6 blue 7 sue + 8 shoe

blue

1 blew 2 brew 3 crew 4 chew 5 drew
6 flew 7 grew 8 sue 9 blue 10 clue 11 flue 12 glue 13 true

1 y 2 oo 3 you 4 few 5 new

1 dew 2 few 3 new 4 pew 5 stew 6 fewer 7 newer
8 stewing 9 due 10 cue 11 queue

1 oo 2 you 3 sue 4 new 5 flew 6 few 7 flue 8 cue
9 crew 10 clue 11 chew 12 grew 13 glue 14 dew 15 due 16 shoe
17 blew 18 pew 19 clue 20 queue 21 stew 22 fewer 23 true

1 zoom 2 bloom 3 blue 4 blew 5 sue 6 soon 7 stew
8 you 9 few 10 fewer 11 roof 12 flew 13 too 14 stool 15 true
16 newer 17 chewing 18 queuing 19 do 20 dew 21 go 22 grew

blue		brew		clue		queue	
glue		grew		crew		queue	
drew		true		sue		shoe	
crew		clue		newer		fewer	
few		dew		too		true	
due		new		boo		blue	
few		pew		flew		few	

true   blue   crew   few   new

_____   _____   _____   _____   _____

4
Find and circle the words

while swimming care fishing cycle repairs beware way wait
bookshop   queues

Beware two way Traffic

NO FISHING NO SWIMMING

the bookshop is open

straight ahead!
next to the fish shop

Do not queue on road ← P

SHOE REPAIRS KEYS CUT WHILE YOU WAIT

Queues likely

10 mph

Cycle With Care

5
Read, then listen and check

too	blue	you	stew	shoe	
pair	re	repair	ware	be	Beware!

6
Add the key words, then listen and check

for   which   an   the   no   doing   in   she

a about am _____ and & at @ be been bit born but by can count day
did do _____ don't down drink each eat English first _____ from get
go going got had he her here Hi him how if I _____ it just let lot may
me mean morning much must near nice _____ not now OK on or out
please pound read room saw say see seen _____ shop so soon than
that _____ them this too up us we went we're when _____ while
with won't word yes you your

7
Dictation

1 _____ _____   2 _____ _____

3 _____ _____   4 _____ _____

~ E L L ~ I L L

1
Read and say

1 b**ell**   2 b**ill**   3 b**all**   4 b**ull**

football

1 ell   2 bell   3 cell   4 fell   5 hell   6 sell
7 tell   8 well   9 shell   10 smell   11 spell

1 ill   2 bill   3 cill   4 fill   5 hill   6 kill   7 mill   8 pill   9 quill
10 till   11 still   12 skill   13 will   14 grill   15 chill   16 silly   17 villa

1 or   2 all   3 ball   4 call   5 fall   6 hall   7 mall   8 tall   9 wall
10 small   11 stall   12 squall

1 ull   2 bull   3 full   4 pull

1 all   2 ill   3 bill   4 ball   5 bell   6 bull   7 fill   8 fall   9 fell
10 full   11 pill   12 pull   13 spell   14 spill   15 small   16 smell   17 skill
18 grill   19 well   20 wall   21 will   22 hill   23 hall   24 hell

2
Listen and tick

ill		all		till		tell	
bell		ball		tall		tell	
ball		bill		hill		hall	
bull		bill		pull		pill	
will		well		smell		small	
wall		well		spell		spill	
fall		full		skill		squall	

3
Trace and write

will   well   small   pull   all   PULL

____   ____   ____   ____   ____

4
Read and label

bell   pills   bull   wall   shell

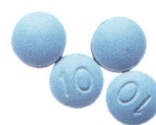

1_____   2_____   3_____   4_____   5_____

baseball Toronto Blue Jays	football Chelsea	football Aston Villa	American football New York Jets
rugby football Bradford Bulls	football Blackburn Rovers	American football Dallas Cowboys	basketball Atlanta Hawks

football	foot • ball	baseball	
basketball	bas • ket • ball	rugby	
Bradford		cowboy	
Blackburn Rovers		Aston Villa	
Chelsea FC		Atlanta Hawks	

① pull ② pulling ③ will ④ willing ⑤ grilling ⑥ smelling ⑦ spelling ⑧ small ⑨ smaller ⑩ tall ⑪ taller ⑫ calling ⑬ caller ⑭ full ⑮ fuller ⑯ kill ⑰ cell ⑱ call ⑲ sell ⑳ falling ㉑ filling

① _____ ② _____ _____
③ _____ _____ _____ ④ _____ _____

~ I G H T   ~ O U G H T

1
Read and say

1 I   **2** my   **3** ite   **4** yte   **5** ight

1 fight **2** light **3** might **4** night **5** right
6 sight **7** tight **8** bright **9** flight **10** fright
11 slight **12** midnight + **13** high **14** sigh
15 height **16** sign

midnight

1 or **2** sort **3** fort **4** fought **5** caught + **6** ate **7** eight **8** 8
9 wait **10** weight

1 fight **2** fought **3** taught **4** tight **5** nought **6** night
7 light **8** right **9** bright **10** flight **11** fright **12** caught
13 midnight **14** ought **15** bought **16** height **17** weight **18** sigh
19 sight **20** sign **21** might **22** eight **23** brought **24** high
25 neighbour

1 ought **2** bought **3** fought **4** nought **5** brought
6 caught **7** taught **8** weight **9** eight **10** eighteen **11** weigh
12 neighbour

2
Listen and tick

light		right		hate		height	
flight		fright		white		weight	
might		night		late		light	
bought		brought		hay		high	
weigh		weight		sin		sign	
eight		weight		say		sigh	
caught		taught		fight		fought	

3
Tick (✓) the same
sounds and cross
(✗) the different
sounds

mate / might	✗	wait / weight	✓
1 fort / fought	☐	**5** fit / fight	☐
2 height / weight	☐	**6** eighteen / eighty	☐
3 ate / eight	☐	**7** Kate / caught	☐
4 Hi / high	☐	**8** cart / caught	☐

0	nought
18	eighteen
80	eighty
40	forty

right   weight   caught   bought

night	night	*night*	**might**	*NIGHT*
right	*night*	right	*Right*	right
brought	*bought*	bought	*bought*	bought
weight	weight	WEIGHT	weight	weigh
CAUGHT	taught	*caught*	caught	caught

→ **East-West Airways** | **boarding pass**

```
Name: Jill Hall      Flight: EW88
From: London Heliport EGLW
To: Shoreham ESH    (Brighton)
Date: 18 May        Time: 18.40
Gate: 18
Seat #: 8 A
Weight of bags:      18 kilos
```

Please wait until we call your flight

Sign Here!

→ **East-West Airways** | **boarding pass**

```
Name: Jill Hall      _____: EW88
From: London Heliport EGLW
To: Shoreham ESH    (Brighton)
_____: 18 May     Time: 18.40
_____: 18
Seat #: 8 A
_____  of bags:  18 kilos
```

Please _____ until we call your _____

WHEN RED LIGHT SHOWS WAIT **HERE**

a night flight   drive on the right   eighty-eight
a midnight flight   please sign here   eighteen forty
day and night   I bought eight   a great weight
goodnight   a bright light   a great height

U ~ E

1 mad 2 m**a**de 3 quit 4 qu**ite** 5 not
6 n**o**te 7 cub 8 c**u**be

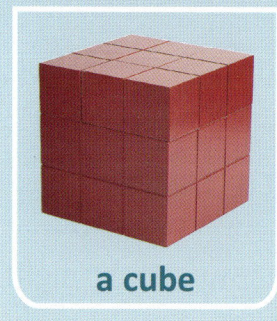
a cube

1 **new** 2 **few** 3 **cue** 4 **cube**
5 **cub** 6 **ice cube**

1 cub 2 cube 3 cut 4 cute 5 dud 6 dude 7 duck
8 duke 9 dun 10 dune 11 tub 12 tube 13 tun 14 tune
15 us 16 use 17 fuse 18 June 19 muse 20 music 21 amuse
22 reduce

1 **rude** 2 **rule** 3 **Luke** 4 **lute** 5 **flute** 6 **fluke**
7 **crude** 8 **prude** 9 **prune** 10 **ruler**

1 hop 2 hope 3 wit 4 white 5 lit 6 light 7 Sam 8 same
9 hot 10 hotel 11 us 12 use 13 cut 14 cute 15 luck 16 Luke
17 few 18 due 19 dune 20 duck 21 duke 22 fade 23 hate
24 site 25 sit 26 sight 27 cub 28 club 29 cube 30 fuse 31 music
32 amuse 33 ruler

too ☐ blue ☐ true ☐ luck ☐ Luke ☐

Sand Dunes →

dot		dote		lute		flute	
pin		pine		prune		prude	
pan		pane		rude		crude	
cub		cube		Luke		fluke	
tub		tube		fool		rule	
us		use		use		fuse	
cut		cute		muse		amuse	

use   rule   rude   tune   music

_____ _____ _____ _____ _____

🌐 website 📠 inbox 📧 e-mail 🖨 print ⏳ time 18:10 ℹ date 18 June

My menu

Music
- songs
- artists
- blues
- jazz

Podcasts

iTunes store

YouTube
- music
- funny clips
- cute kids

YouTube

iTunes music

Toast: burn CDs

eBay: buy and sell on the net

✈ flight tracker
Airline:
British Airways BA003
From: New York
To: London
➡ CHECK NOW

🌐 world time
Hong Kong: 02:10
London: 18:10
New York: 13:10

❄ world weather
Hong Kong: cloudy
London: storms
New York: windy

5 🔴
Find the new words and circle them, then listen and check

1 by 2 buy 3 burn 4 music 5 iTunes 6 YouTube
7 reduce speed now

6 🔴
Read, then listen and check

iTunes music
tunes from a website
download a tune

buy on eBay
sell on eBay
a good new rule

a ruler
a new ruler
a new blue ruler

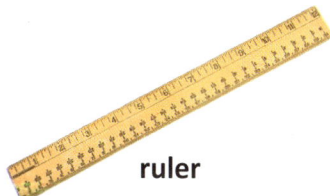
ruler

1
Read and say

1 cab 2 cable 3 tab 4 table
5 bib 6 bible 7 rif 8 rifle

apple

1 able 2 cable 3 fable 4 gable 5 table
6 bible 7 rifle 8 title 9 cradle 10 needle
11 noodle 12 google 13 beetle 14 Beatles

1 gab 2 gable 3 tap 4 apple 5 set 6 settle
7 gig 8 giggle 9 hob 10 hobble 11 mud
12 muddle 13 dazzle

1 apple 2 battle 3 cattle 4 raffle 5 paddle 6 dazzle
7 cripple 8 fiddle 9 giggle 10 little 11 middle 12 ripple
13 sizzle 14 drizzle 15 griddle 16 kettle 17 settle 18 bottle
19 wobble 20 goggle 21 bubble 22 cuddle 23 muddle
24 puddle 25 rubble 26 shuttle

1 table 2 tattle 3 title 4 little 5 rifle 6 middle 7 cattle
8 kettle 9 sizzle 10 shuttle 11 google 12 muddle 13 noodle
14 able 15 apple

2
Listen and tick

able		table		rubber		rubble	
need		needle		litter		little	
beat		Beatle		battle		bottle	
google		goggle		griddle		giggle	
muddle		puddle		middle		muddle	
dazzle		drizzle		raffle		rifle	
cattle		kettle		noodle		needle	

3
Trace and write

little   table   title   middle   bottle

_____   _____   _____   _____   _____

4
Read and label

bottle	kettle	table	rifle	cable

1 _____ 2 _____ 3 _____ 4 _____ 5 _____

5
Find the new words and circle them

-US:official&sa=N&imgsz=   🔍 disabled parking

Recent Searches
disabled parking
bottle banks
Apple Records
The Beatles
cable tv
kettles and griddles
book titles
space shuttle
cable TV

Clear Recent Searches

Google

Results 1-10   disabled p

table 1: baby dept		
sales	this year	next year
kettles	340	310
cradles	290	410
bottles	15,000	14,000

SPACE SHUTTLE

6
Read, then listen and check

cable TV	space shuttle	a little bit more
google 'noodle'	Apple Records	a little bottle
Apple Mac	The Beatles	a kettle on the table
puddle in the middle	sizzle on the griddle	apple on the table

1 _____ _____ _____ _____

2 _____ _____ _____ _____

3 _____ _____ 4 _____ _____ _____

7
Dictation

8
Find words from Unit 46

T	F	F	Q	M	J	A	E	N	T
I	A	D	R	I	Z	Z	L	E	A
T	B	X	G	D	P	L	O	E	B
L	L	P	A	D	D	L	E	D	L
E	E	X	B	L	R	I	F	L	E
A	P	P	L	E	G	R	Z	E	A
B	O	B	E	M	U	D	D	L	E
L	B	O	T	T	L	E	K	M	H
E	L	N	G	I	G	G	L	E	L

BROWN GLASS BOTTLES & JARS

95

~ O L D   ~ O U L D

1
Read and say

1 **odd**   2 **goal**   3 **old**   4 **cold**
5 **gold**   6 **older**   7 **boulder**
8 **shoulder**

folder

1 **old**   2 **bold**   3 **cold**   4 **fold**   5 **gold**   6 **hold**   7 **sold**   8 **told**
9 **mould**   10 **older**   11 **folder**   12 **colder**   13 **boulder**   14 **shoulder**

1 **good**   2 **wood**   3 **could**   4 **would**   5 **should**

1 **cold**   2 **could**   3 **sold**   4 **should**   5 **shoulder**   6 **good**
7 **gold**   8 **told**   9 **bold**   10 **wood**   11 **would**   12 **mould**   13 **hold**
14 **fold**   15 **folder**   16 **older**   17 **colder**   18 **bold**   19 **hood**   20 **boulder**
21 **mouldy**   22 **folding**   23 **holding**

2
Number from 1–7

old ☐   told ☐   older ☐   shoulder ☐1   should ☐   could ☐   would ☐

3
Listen and tick

fold		folder		shoulder		should	
cold		colder		word		would	
bold		boulder		cord		could	
goal		gold		card		could	
cod		cold		world		would	
Tod		told		shoe		should	
hod		hold		shade		should	

4
Tick (✓) the same sounds and cross (✗) the different sounds

would / boulder ☒   sold / shoulder ☑

1 could / mould ☐   5 shout / should ☐
2 should / wood ☐   6 could / hood ☐
3 boulder / shoulder ☐   7 could / should ☐
4 would / fold ☐   8 would / hold ☐

~ O L D ~ O U L D

old   sold   should   would   could

_____ _____ _____ _____ _____

1 moon 2 June 3 good 4 would 5 shoot 6 shout 7 shoulder
8 should 9 cold 10 could 11 hood 12 noodle 13 needle 14 bold 15 bolder
16 boulder 17 fold 18 too 19 tune 20 tub 21 tube 22 told

old gold coin	ice-cold drink	a cold wood
old shoulder bag	nice cold drink	an old wood
falling boulders	sold a cold drink	a good old wood
Beware! Falling boulders!	ice-cold drinks sold here	an old cold wood

Would you like a hot drink or a cold drink?

I would like a cold drink.

Would you like ice?

Yes, I would.

J	Z	S	E	S	O	L	D
P	S	H	O	U	L	D	F
U	W	O	K	F	D	C	O
W	O	U	L	D	G	O	L
H	O	L	D	G	C	U	D
O	D	D	X	O	O	L	E
O	Y	E	B	O	L	D	R
D	Q	R	A	D	D	U	O

cold woods

ice-cold drink

a new gold coin

an old shoulder bag

Beware!
Falling boulders

5
Trace and write

6
Read, then listen and check

7
Find and circle words from Unit 47, then listen and check

8
Find words from Unit 47

T H   T H   ~

1 **th** 2 **th**an 3 **th**at 4 **th**em
5 **th**en 6 **th**is 7 wi**th** 8 ga**th**er
9 fur**th**er 10 brea**th**e 11 soo**th**e

33

thirty-three

1 **th** 2 **th** 3 **th**ank 4 **th**ing
5 mou**th** 6 nor**th**

1 thick 2 thin 3 think 4 thing 5 thank 6 three 7 thirteen
8 thirty 9 third 10 thorn 11 thaw 12 thought 13 thirsty
14 thrill

1 mouth 2 south 3 north 4 tooth 5 teeth 6 birth
7 breath 8 youth 9 both 10 maths

1 **th**in 2 **th**ick 3 **th**is 4 **th**ing 5 **th**an 6 **th**ank 7 brea**th**e
8 brea**th** 9 fur**th**er 10 bir**th**

1 think 2 **th**in 3 three 4 teeth 5 thought 6 north
7 south 8 soothe 9 thirty 10 further 11 youth 12 both
13 birth 14 thought 15 this

tan		than		too		tooth	
ten		then		toot		tooth	
his		this		tea		teeth	
wit		with		nor		north	
soon		soothe		torn		thorn	
take		thank		boat		both	
tea		three		mat		math	
third		thirty		Bert		birth	
thirty		thirsty		nought		north	

1 _3_   2 ___   3 ___   4 ___   5 ___   6 ___   7 ___

thank this both with them

_____ _____ _____ _____ _____

4
Trace and write

1 too 2 tooth 3 tea 4 teeth 5 bought 6 thought
7 fur 8 further 9 porch 10 north 11 out 12 south 13 that
14 gather 15 born 16 birth 17 three 18 third 19 thirty
20 thirsty 21 breath 22 breathe

Think bike

5
Read, say and check

TO
SOUTH NORTH
INTERSTATE INTERSTATE
NEVADA NEVADA
15 15

north-west   north

west   north-east

south-west   NW N NE
W E
SW S SE

east

south   south-east

6
Find words from Unit 48, then listen and check

First name: _Kathy_

Surname: _Thatcher_

Date of birth: _13th June, 1983_

Place of birth: _Southampton_

7
Find more words from Unit 48, then listen and check

- with / both / birth / date of birth / place of birth
- than / thank / that / the / them / this / thing
- three / third / thirteen / thirty / thirteenth
- can / could / will / would / should / may / might

8
Read the key words, then listen and check

1 **2** **1** ST **2** ND

① **bun** ② **fun** ③ **gun** ④ **sun**
⑤ **won** ⑥ **son** ⑦ **one** ⑧ **1**
⑨ **come** ⑩ **some**

ONE WAY ➡

① **to** ② **too** ③ **you** ④ **do** ⑤ **queue**
⑥ **two** ⑦ **2**

① **one** ② **two** ③ **three** ④ **four** ⑤ **five** ⑥ **six** ⑦ **seven**
⑧ **eight** ⑨ **nine** ⑩ **ten** ⑪ **eleven** ⑫ **twelve** ⑬ **thirteen**
⑭ **fourteen** ⑮ **fifteen** ⑯ **sixteen** ⑰ **seventeen** ⑱ **eighteen**
⑲ **nineteen** ⑳ **twenty** ㉑ **thirty** ㉒ **forty** ㉓ **fifty**

① **1ˢᵗ / first** ② **2ⁿᵈ / second** ③ **3ʳᵈ /third** ④ **4ᵗʰ /fourth**
⑤ **5ᵗʰ / fifth** ⑥ **6ᵗʰ / sixth** ⑦ **7ᵗʰ / seventh** ⑧ **8ᵗʰ / eighth**
⑨ **9ᵗʰ / ninth** ⑩ **10ᵗʰ / tenth** ⑪ **11ᵗʰ / eleventh**
⑫ **12ᵗʰ / twelfth** ⑬ **13ᵗʰ / thirteenth**

① **win** ② **on** ③ **won** ④ **one** ⑤ **toe** ⑥ **too** ⑦ **top** ⑧ **to** ⑨ **two**
⑩ **you** ⑪ **rum** ⑫ **gum** ⑬ **come** ⑭ **sum** ⑮ **some** ⑯ **home** ⑰ **son**
⑱ **one** ⑲ **two** ⑳ **2ⁿᵈ** ㉑ **3ʳᵈ** ㉒ **1ˢᵗ** ㉓ **4ᵗʰ** ㉔ **9ᵗʰ** ㉕ **5ᵗʰ** ㉖ **12ᵗʰ**

fir		first		thirteen		thirty	
thirst		first		fourteen		forty	
thirst		first		fifteen		fifty	
for		fourth		sixteen		sixty	
fist		fifth		seventeen		seventy	
six		sixth		eighteen		eighty	
seven		seventh		nineteen		ninety	
eleven		eleventh		fifteen		fifteenth	
twelve		twelfth		nineteen		nineteenth	

1 ST   2 ND   3 RD   4 TH   5 TH

___ ___ ___ ___ ___

4 Match the numbers with the spaces

5 Find the different word

6 Fill in the missing numbers

7 Read, then listen and circle the words you hear

1st 2nd 3rd 4th 5th 6th 7th 8th 9th 10th 11th 12th 13th

1 third ____	2 tenth ____	3 sixth ____	4 thirteenth ____
5 ninth ____	6 second ____	7 twelfth ____	8 fourth ____
9 eleventh ____	10 fifth ____	11 first ____	12 eighth ____

third	*third*	*third*	thirty	THIRD
fifth	five	fifth	*fifth*	fifth
one	**one**	one	ONE	on
two	twin	two	*two*	*TWO*
second	seventh	seventh	seventh	**SEVENTH**

1 one two _____ four _____ six seven _____ nine ten

2 _____ second third _____ _____ sixth _____ eighth ninth _____

3 one _____ five seven nine _____ thirteen _____

4 two four _____ eight ten _____ _____ sixteen

5 1st _____ 3rd 4th _____ 6th _____ 8th _____ 10th

6 ten _____ thirty forty _____ sixty seventy _____ ninety

Lift
maximum twelve persons

floors	
10 tenth	bank, cashpoint
9 ninth	book shop
8 eighth	TVs, DVDs, CDs
7 seventh	tables, chairs
6 sixth	cups, plates
5 fifth	men
4 fourth	boys and girls, toys
3 third	ladies
2 second	perfume, make-up
1 first	coffee shop
0 ground	supermarket
↑ UP	↓ DOWN

Two great places to eat!

RESTAURANT on the first floor

WE LOVE COFFEE

COFFEE LOUNGE on the ground floor

50

S T R   S P R   S C R

1
Read and say

1 s 2 say 3 st 4 stay 5 str 6 stray

7 s 8 sing 9 sp 10 spin 11 spr 12 spring

13 s 14 see 15 sc 16 scan 17 scr 18 screen

screw

1 strap 2 stray 3 strain 4 straight
5 street 6 stream 7 strip 8 stripe 9 strife 10 strike
11 striker 12 string 13 stroll 14 strong 15 strum 16 struck
17 struggle 18 astra

1 sprat 2 spray 3 sprain 4 spring 5 sprite 6 sprout
7 sprung 8 spry

1 scrap 2 scrape 3 scream 4 screen 5 screw 6 script
7 scroll 8 scrum 9 scruffy

1 stray 2 spray 3 spring 4 string 5 screw 6 street
7 screen 8 strong 9 scroll 10 straight

2
Listen and tick

rain		train		cream		scream	
train		strain		seem		scream	
steam		stream		crew		screw	
sting		string		pry		spry	
trip		strip		pray		spray	
truck		struck		tray		stray	
trike		strike		treat		street	

3
Trace and write

street   spring   screen   straight

_____ _____ _____ _____

4
Read and label

string   screwdriver   strap   spring   screen

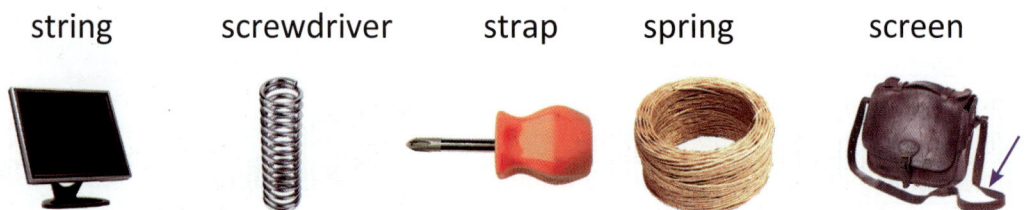

1_____ 2_____ 3_____ 4_____ 5_____

1 ex   2 extra   3 extreme   4 explain   5 express

1 crew   2 screw   3 press   4 express   5 pray   6 spray   7 seen   8 screen
9 skip   10 rip   11 script   12 song   13 strong   14 roll   15 scroll   16 eight   17 straight
18 scrape   19 pain   20 rain   21 sprain   22 cream   23 seem   24 scream   25 striker
26 astra   27 extra   28 plain   29 explain

an express train	a striker	extra ice, please
an express bus	an extra striker	a Sprite, please
a shuttle bus	South Street	a Sprite with extra ice, please
an express shuttle bus	North Street	scroll up the screen

SOUTH STREET

WEST STREET

SHORT STAY CHARGES
DAY TICKETS
8.00am - 7.00pm (Mon - Sat)
20 Mins   20p
1 Hour   40p
2 Hours   80p

EXPRESS Shuttle

Poole
Bournemouth
London
£15 Day Return

go for less, 15 times a day

for tickets and information
GoByCoach.com

Extra ICE
SUGARFREE GUM
SCIENTIFICALLY PROVEN...
GB available

scroll bar

ASTRA

5
Read, say and check

6
Read, then listen and check

7
Find and circle words from Unit 50

~ N G L E   ~ N D L E

1
Read and say

1 giggle 2 cradle 3 needle 4 middle
5 wobble 6 bubble 7 ripple 8 cripple

candle

1 bang 2 bangle 3 angle
4 strangle 5 jingle 6 single
7 bungle 8 jungle 9 try 10 triangle

1 can 2 canned 3 candle 4 hand 5 handle
6 spin 7 spindle 8 fond 9 fondle 10 bundle

1 ram 2 ramble 3 scramble 4 tremble
5 bumble 6 rumble 7 crumble 8 grumble
9 thimble 10 amble

1 amp 2 ample 3 sample 4 example 5 trample
6 dimple 7 pimple 8 simple 9 rumple 10 crumple

2
Listen and tick

amble		ample		crumple		crumble	
ample		angle		jungle		jingle	
tremble		trample		dimple		pimple	
crumble		grumble		strangle		scramble	
single		simple		ample		example	
rumble		ramble		thimble		spindle	
bundle		bumble		sample		simple	

3
Trace and write

example   grumble   handle   single

4
Read and label

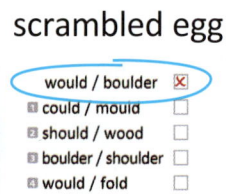

jungle   candles   example   scrambled egg   a bundle

would / boulder ☒
1 could / mould ☐
2 should / wood ☐
3 boulder / shoulder ☐
4 would / fold ☐

1_____ 2_____ 3_____ 4_____ 5_____

1 tria_____   2 ca_____   3 tre_____   4 exa_____   5 bu_____

6 si_____   7 si_____   8 gru_____   9 ju_____   10 sa_____

5 🔴
Listen, write in
ngle / *ndle* / *mble*
/ *mple*

DRAW & PAINT PROGRAM

DRAW SHAPES >>

triangle

square

cube

circle

line

curve

angle   15°

star

speech
bubble

6 🔴
Find and circle
words you know,
then listen and
check

birthday	*birth • day*	CD single	
candles		example	
bumblebee		simple	
scrambled egg		apple crumble	
triangle		right angle (90°)	
sample a song		jungle drums	

7 🔴
Mark the syllables,
then listen and
check

a warning triangle

Single
track
road
Use passing
places
to permit
overtaking

~ G E G E ~

1 rag 2 rage 3 wag 4 wage
5 stag 6 stage 7 ace 8 pace
9 age 10 page 11 race 12 rage

a German car

1 age 2 cage 3 page 4 rage 5 sage 6 stage
7 wage 8 hug 9 huge 10 get 11 gent 12 ginger

1 gel 2 gent 3 germ 4 German 5 Germany
6 gem 7 gene 8 general 9 gentle

1 agent 2 agency 3 image 4 village 5 gym
6 gypsum 7 Egypt 8 surgery 9 advantage

1 Jim 2 gym 3 Jem 4 gem 5 jingle 6 gin 7 ginger 8 Jenny
9 general 10 wage 11 stage 12 gent 13 agent 14 image 15 huge
16 gene 17 gym 18 Egypt 19 page 20 age 21 surgery

stag		stage		agent		agency	
rag		rage		a gym		Egypt	
wag		wage		glaze		age	
a mag		image		gram		germ	
get		gent		hug		huge	
stool		stooge		bug		budge	
gain		Jane		green		gene	

wage   huge   gentle   gym   surgery

_____ _____ _____ _____ _____

cage   gym   pages   Egypt   Germany

1 _____ 2 _____ 3 _____ 4 _____ 5 _____

4
Read and label

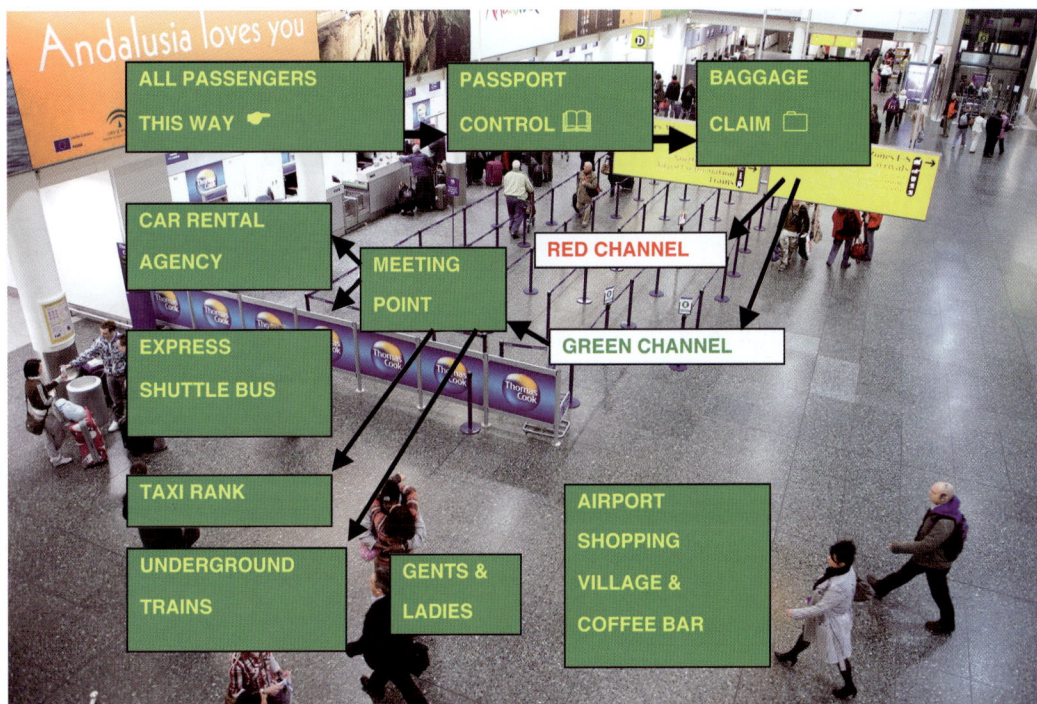

5
Find and circle the Gs, then put these words in the box with the same *g* sound

g in *got*	
g in *gel*	passengers
g in *sing*	

1 get 2 gem 3 jet 4 gym 5 Jenny 6 German 7 huge 8 hugging
9 surgery 10 cage 11 stag 12 stagger 13 stage 14 general 15 gel 16 pace
17 pack 18 pain 19 page 20 rage 21 bag 22 age 23 baggage

6
Read, then listen and check

a village in Germany   travel agency   excess baggage
going to Egypt   car rental agency   air passengers
baggage claim   germs in the surgery   underground train

o O U O W

1
Read and say

1 **how** 2 **now** 3 **cow** 4 **down**
5 **town** 6 **brown** 7 **frown**
8 **tower** 9 **flower** 10 **shower**
11 **out** 12 **our** 13 **ours**

SLOW DOWN 30

1 **now** 2 **out** 3 **no** 4 **road** 5 **toe** 6 **open** 7 **home**
8 **low** 9 **slow** 10 **grow**

1 **low** 2 **blow** 3 **crow** 4 **grow** 5 **grown** 6 **show** 7 **slow**
8 **slower** 9 **throw** 10 **flow** 11 **flown** 12 **glow** 13 **pillow**
14 **window** 15 **yellow** 16 **willow**

1 **no** 2 **so** 3 **go** 4 **coat** 5 **woe** 6 **note** 7 **vote** 8 **zone**
9 **smoke** 10 **smoking** 11 **close** 12 **closed** 13 **OK** 14 **open**
15 **hotel** 16 **solo** 17 **video** 18 **radio** 19 **Coca-Cola** 20 **post**
21 **o'clock** 22 **Microsoft**

1 **now** 2 **slow** 3 **snow** 4 **show** 5 **how** 6 **shower** 7 **grow**
8 **grown** 9 **glow** 10 **throw** 11 **thrown** 12 **OK** 13 **Oh!** 14 **open**
15 **closed** 16 **window** 17 **down** 18 **solo** 19 **radio** 20 **our** 21 **boat**
22 **coat** 23 **out** 24 **so** 25 **ours** 26 **town**

2
Listen and tick

no		now		town		thrown	
rod		road		window		willow	
brown		blown		tower		flower	
it's snow		it's now		willow		yellow	
our		over		show her		shower	
a pen		open		grow		glow	
slow		slower		frown		flown	

3
Trace and write

how   now   our   slow   yellow

_____ _____ _____ _____ _____

4
Read and label

5
Find the sounds

6
Read, then listen
and check

red　　blue　　green　　yellow　　black　　brown

| 1 _____ | 2 _____ | 3 _____ | 4 _____ | 5 _____ | 6 _____ |

o in *vote, boat*	road closed
o in *got, not*	
o in *cow*	

1 now　2 no　3 note　4 boat　5 so　6 slow　7 shower　8 how　9 our　10 yell
11 yellow　12 pill　13 pillow　14 post　15 o'clock　16 OK　17 out　18 go

out of town	closed, open at ten	Radio One
no smoking	Post Office	Microsoft Windows
road closed	Bay Hotel	slow down
Yellow Pages	outdoor pool	down and out

P H ~ G H

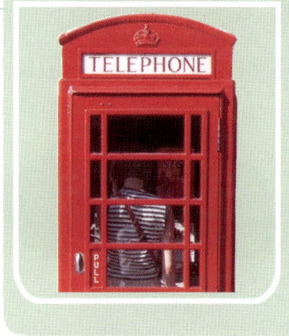

1 **fox** 2 **foam** 3 **fin** 4 **fine**
5 **bone** 6 **ph**one 7 **ph**oto

1 **phone** 2 **telephone** 3 **photo** 4 **phono**
5 **phrase** 6 **physics** 7 **physical** 8 **phantom**
9 **pharmacy** 10 **Philip** 11 **photocopy**

1 al**ph**a 2 al**ph**abet 3 s**ph**ere 4 gra**ph** 5 **ph**otogra**ph**
6 ne**ph**ew 7 ty**ph**oid

1 **laugh** (larf) 2 **cough** (coff) 3 **rough** (ruff)
4 **tough** (tuff) 5 **enough** (eenuff)

1 **phone** 2 **alphabet** 3 **photo** 4 **graph** 5 **nephew** 6 **rough**
7 **physics** 8 **tough** 9 **pharmacy** 10 **cough** 11 **photograph**

photo		hotel		rough		tough	
phone		phono		cough		coffee	
phrase		raise		laugh		lark	
phone		foam		tough		touch	
phone		home		graph		grape	
sphere		spear		nephew		a few	
graph		grant		enough		a nut	

phone   photo   graph   laugh   enough

_____ _____ _____ _____ _____

graph   alphabet   phantom   sphere   photo

 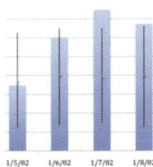 ABCDEFG HIJKLMN OPQRST UVWXYZ

1 _____ 2 _____ 3 _____ 4 _____ 5 _____

1 graph 2 laugh 3 off 4 cough 5 tough 6 stuff 7 alpha 8 alphabet
9 foot 10 photo 11 foam 12 phone 13 few 14 nephew 15 boy 16 foil 17 try
18 typhoid 19 queer 20 spear 21 here 22 sphere 23 fizz 24 physics

■ or / for / your / ought / born
■ now / how / our / ours / pound / count / down
■ no / go / so / slow / phone / photo / o'clock / OK
■ good / wood / could / should / would
■ not / off / soft / cough

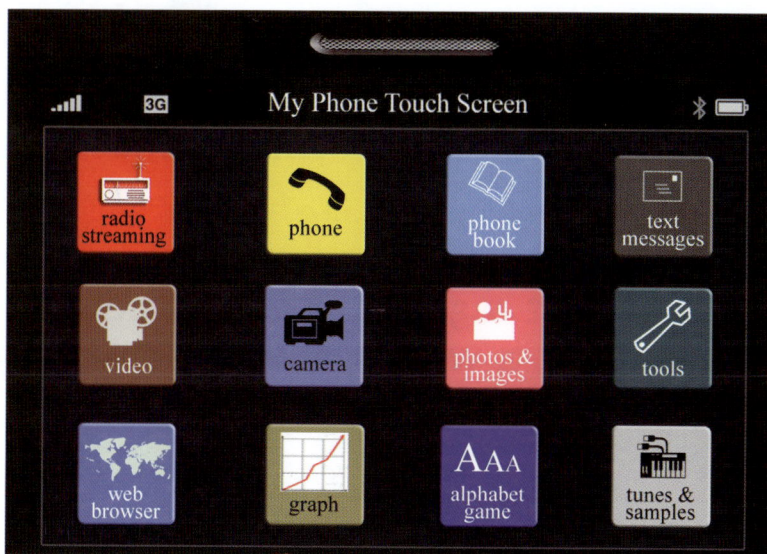

My Phone Touch Screen

radio streaming | phone | phone book | text messages
video | camera | photos & images | tools
web browser | graph | AAA alphabet game | tunes & samples

can   while   ought   enough   must   thank   in   be

a able about all am an and & at @ _____ been birth bit born both
but _____ come could count day did do doing don't down drink each
eat English _____ first for from get go going got had he her here
Hi him how if I _____ it just let little lot may me mean might morning
much _____ near nice night no not now o'clock OK on or _____ our
ours out phone photo please pound read room saw say see seen she
shop should slow so some soon than _____ that the them thing this
too up us we well went we're when which _____ will with won't word
would yes you your yours

1 _____ 2 _____ 3 _____ 4 _____ 5 _____

5
Read, say and check

6
Find and circle words from Units 51–54, then listen and check

7
Add the key words, then listen and check

8
Dictation

| K | N | G | N | W | R | W | H |

1 Read and say

1 **not** 2 **knot** 3 **new** 4 **knew**
5 **no** 6 **know** 7 **Nat** 8 **gnat**

knot

1 **knack** 2 **knee** 3 **knit** 4 **knife** 5 **knight**
6 **knickers** 7 **know** 8 **knew** 9 **knot**
10 **knock** 11 **knit** 12 **knuckle** 13 **gnat** 14 **gnash** 15 **gnaw**

1 **ring** 2 **wring** 3 **rap** 4 **wrap** 5 **right**
6 **write** 7 **wrangler** 8 **wren** 9 **wreck**
10 **wrong** 11 **wrinkle** 12 **writer** 13 **writing**
14 **wrote** 15 **wrench** 16 **wrist**

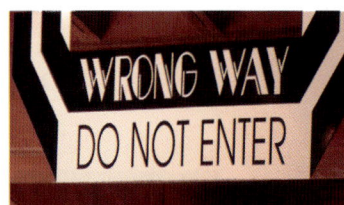

1 **our** 2 **hour** 3 **honour** 4 **do** 5 **who** 6 **whose** 7 **whom**
8 **hole** 9 **whole**

1 **knife** 2 **write** 3 **knit** 4 **gnat** 5 **wrap** 6 **knock** 7 **knee**
8 **knuckle** 9 **wrinkle** 10 **wrong** 11 **know** 12 **who** 13 **hour**
14 **whole** 15 **whose**

2 Listen and tick

knot		knock		gnat		knack	
ring		wrong		gnaw		know	
know		knew		gnash		gash	
knife		night		knew		cue	
how		hour		knot		cot	
who		whose		wing		wring	
who		whom		write		writer	

3 Trace and write

know   wrong   gnat   hour   whose

____   ____   ____   ____   ____

4 Read and label

knee   two hours   wrist   gnat   knife

1 _____ 2 _____ 3 _____ 4 _____ 5 _____

1 right 2 write 3 ring 4 wring 5 wrong 6 nice 7 knife 8 need 9 knee 10 ours 11 hours 12 hoot 13 whom 14 blue 15 screw 16 do 17 who 18 you 19 whose 20 pole 21 whole 22 home 23 know 24 queue 25 dew 26 knew 27 not 28 knot 29 knock 30 wrote 31 wrangler 32 writing 33 reading

- night / write / right / might
- hi / how / him / here / he / her / who / whose
- no / not / now / near / nice / know / knew
- read / room / wrong / write / wrote / right
- I / know / how / to / read / and / write / now

write   knuckle   white   write   gnat   hour

1 knife 2 wrong 3 whole 4 gnaw 5 gnash 6 knew 7 knock 8 wrote 9 wrinkle 10 when

key / knee	☒	right / write	☑		
1 ring / wring	☐	5 no / know	☐	9 home / whom	☐
2 Wong / wrong	☐	6 kit / knit	☐	10 how / hour	☐
3 white / write	☐	7 hole / whole	☐	11 not / knot	☐
4 new / knew	☐	8 when / wren	☐	12 hose / whose	☐

Z	W	R	E	C	K	J	U
W	R	A	P	K	N	E	E
R	I	W	G	N	O	W	H
I	T	R	N	I	W	H	O
S	E	O	A	F	I	O	U
T	M	N	W	E	N	S	R
D	Y	G	N	A	T	E	K
W	H	O	L	E	G	N	N

writing

reading

5 🔴
Read, say and check

6 🔴
Read, then listen and check

7
Listen and highlight the silent letters

8
Tick (✓) the same sounds and cross (✗) the different sounds

9
Find words from Unit 55

E A   A I   E Y   E I R

1 **be** 2 **been** 3 **bean** 4 **each**
5 **tea** 6 **teach** 7 **teacher**
8 **team** 9 **cheap** 10 **stream**
11 **pay** 12 **paid** 13 **made**

bread

1 **bed** 2 **bred** 3 **bread** 4 **head** 5 **dead** 6 **tread** 7 **said**

1 **may** 2 **say** 3 **they** 4 **grey** 5 **air** 6 **share** 7 **their** 8 **there**

1 **hot** 2 **knot** 3 **what** 4 **was** 5 **want**
6 **her** 7 **hers** 8 **fur** 9 **girl** 10 **were**
11 **car** 12 **far** 13 **are**

This is
Car Park B
and you are
on Level 3

B3

1 **fire** 2 **wire** 3 **spire** 4 **shire** 5 **dire**
6 **flyer** 7 **pyre** 8 **byre** 9 **dryer** 10 **drier**
11 **liar**

1 **beach** 2 **bread** 3 **heel** 4 **heap** 5 **head** 6 **way** 7 **laid**
8 **said** 9 **say** 10 **deal** 11 **dead** 12 **hay** 13 **grey** 14 **pray** 15 **they**
16 **fair** 17 **dare** 18 **their** 19 **here** 20 **were** 21 **there** 22 **are**

hot		what		dire		fire	
they		their		why		wire	
say		said		fly		fire	
may		way		deed		dead	
there		hair		bead		bread	
her		hair		fly		flyer	
are		our		gay		grey	

they   their   was   were   what

_____   _____   _____   _____   _____

fire   grey hair   hairdryer   head   wire-cutters

1_____ 2_____ 3_____ 4_____ 5_____

1 I 2 you 3 he 4 she 5 we 6 they 7 me 8 him 9 her 10 them 11 are 12 was 13 were 14 who 15 what 16 which 17 whose 18 when 19 why 20 want 21 said 22 here 23 there 24 our 25 their 26 right 27 wrong 28 bread

smell when could spin down they soon do now know this sky their bar dear head while light teach her that got born she

tell	smell	beach		town	
we		said		what	
here		would		grey	
who		might		there	
are		slow		June	
were		why		drawn	
how		hat		kiss	
mile		ten		tin	

please when could her soon able

a _____ about all am an and & are at @ be been birth bit born both but can come _____ count day did do doing don't down drink each eat English enough first for from get go going good got had he _____ here Hi him hour how I if in it just know let little lot may me mean might morning much must near nice night no not now o'clock OK on or ought our ours out phone photo _____ pound read room said saw say see seen she shop should slow so some _____ than thank that the their them there they thing this too up us want was we well went were we're what _____ which while who whose will with won't word would write wrong yes you your

4 Read and label

5 Read, then listen and check

6 Match the words in the box with words with the same sound, then listen and check

7 Add the key words, then listen and check

Word list

Unit 2

`A` `T` `I` `N`

an
at
in
it
nan
nat
nit
tan
tat
tin

Unit 3

`E` `P`

pan
pat
pen
pet
pin
pip
pit
tap
ten
tip

Unit 4

`M` `D`

am
dad
dam
did
dim
din
mad
man
map
mat
men
met
pad

Unit 5

`O`

dot
mod
mop
nod
not
on
pod
pop
pot
Tod
Tom
top

Unit 6

`G` `V`

dig
dog
get
gig
God
got
nag
peg
pig
tag
van
vat
vet
vim

Unit 7

`H` `L`

had
hal
halal
hat
hen
hid
him
hit

hop
hot
lap
let
lid
lip
log
lot

Unit 8

`U` `C`

can
cap
cat
cog
cot
cup
cut
gun
hug
hut
mug
nut
pop up
tip up
top up

Unit 9

`B` `S`

bag
bed
beg
big
bin
bit
bug
bun
bus
but
Cab
cub
Deb
hub

sad

sat nav

Seb

set

sip

sit

sum

sun

tub

us

Unit 10

`R`

Arab

rag

ram

ran

rap

rat

red

rep

rid

rig

rim

rip

rob

rod

Ron

rub

rug

run

rut

Unit 11

`Y` `W` `J`

Arabic

Basra

jab

jam

Jan

Japan

Jen

jet

jig

Jim

job

jug

Lebanon

Madrid

web

wet

win

wit

won

yam

yen

yes

yet

yob

Unit 12

`F` `X` `Z`

box

disk

exam

exit

Exxon

fan

fat

fax

fed

Fedex

fig

fit

fix

fizz

fog

fox

fun

if

jazz

Lexus

mix

ox

Oz

sax

sex

six

tax

Texaco

wax

zed

zig zag

Unit 13

`K` `C` `K`

back

backpack

deck

dock

duck

keg

kick

kid

kin

kit

lack

lick

lock

luck

muck

pack

pick

rack

rock

sack

sick

tick

wick

Unit 14

`Q` `U` `T` `H` `W` `H`

quick

quid

quip

quit

than

that

them

then

this

when

whim

whip

whiz

with

Unit 15

`S` `H` `C` `H` `T` `C` `H`

catch

cash

chap

chat

chin

chip

chock

chop

dash

dish

ditch

fetch

fish

hatch

hush

itch

lash

latch

mash

match

much

mush

patch

pitch

posh

sash

shed

shin

ship

shock

shop

shot

shut

such

which

wish

Unit 16

O | O

boo

boo hoo

boom

boot

do

food

fox

hoot

hot

loo

loot

lot

moo

moon

noon

not

Oo

posh

rom

roof

room

root

rot

shoot

shop

shot

sock

soon

too

toot

top

whoosh

zoo

zoom

Unit 17

E | E | E | A

beach

beak

bean

bee

beef

been

cheap

cheek

coffee

each

eat

eel

fee

feed

feet

keen

keep

meat

meet

neat

queen

read

sea

seat

seat

see

seem

seen

sheep

tea

teach

team

teen

ten

week

wheat

wheel

Unit 18

B | E | M | E

be

bee

he

heap

hem

hen

me

sea

she

shed

sheep

we

weep

Unit 19

A | Y | A | I

aid

aim

bay

chain

day

fail

gay

hail

hay

jail

jay

laid

lay

mail
mailbox
main
nail
pain
pay
rail
railway
rain
ray
sail
say
tail
wail
wait
way

Unit 20

| N | O | | O | A | ~ | | O | E | . |

boat
coach
coat
doe
don't
foam
foe
goat
Joe
load
loan
moan
oat
open
road
roam
soak
soap
toe
woe
won't

Unit 21

| A | R |

arc
arm
art
bar

bard
bark
car
card
charm
chart
dark
far
farm
hard
harm
jar
lark
mark
park
part
tart

Unit 22

| S | T | ~ | | ~ | S | T |

beast
best
boast
bust
chest
coast
cost
dust
east
feast
fist
just
least
list
lost
must
rest
roast
rust
stab
stack
stain
star
start
stash
stay
steam
steel

stem
stick
stock
stool
stop
stuck
stun
test
toast
vest
waist
west

Unit 23

| C | R | | T | R |

crack
cram
crash
cream
credit
creep
crest
crick
crop
cross
crossroads
crush
crust
crutch
track
trail
train
tram
trap
trash
travel
tray
treat
tree
trek
trick
troop
trot
truck
trust

Unit 24

| B | R | D | R | F | R | G | R | P | R |

afraid
agree
brain
bran
brash
breed
brick
broom
brush
drag
drain
dream
drip
drop
drum
frail
freak
free
fresh
frock
frog
from
frost
grab
gram
grand
green
greet
grin
grip
grub
pram
pray
prick
proof
prop

Unit 25

| A | ~ | E |

base
brake
brave
cake
cane
case
cave
dam
dame
date
fame
fate
frame
game
gate
gave
grape
grate
grave
hate
Kate
lack
lake
lane
late
laze
mad
made
maid
mane
mate
maze
name
rave
safe
sail
sake
Sal
sale
Sam
same
shack
shake
shape
shave
state
take
tape
wake
wave
whale

Unit 26

| I | ~ | E |

bike
bribe
bride
chime
crime
dim
dime
dine
drive
file
fin
fine
five
hike
I
I'm
lick
life
like
lime
Lin
line
mile
mine
nine
pip
pipe
pipeline
quit
quite
ride
shine
Sid
side
sit
site
tide
Tim
time
tribe
while
white
wide
wife

Unit 27

O	~	E

boat
bone
broke
cod
code
cone
cope
cove
drove
hoe
home
hop
hope
hot
hotel
joke
lone
motel
note
pop
pope
probe
rob
robe
rod
rode
rope
stone
stove
tone
vote
weak
wick
woke
zone

Unit 29

B	L	C	L	F	L	G	L

P	L	S	L

black
bleed
block
bloom
blush
clam

clap
clean
clock
club
flash
flat
flea
float
flock
glad
glen
glum
plan
plane
plate
play
plead
please
sleep
slot
slum

Unit 30

~	N	D	~	N	K	~	N	T

~	N	C	H

and
ant
band
bank
bench
bend
bond
brand
bunch
crunch
don't
drink
end
faint
fond
French
gland
grand
grunt
hand
Hank
hint

inch
ink
junk
land
lend
link
lunch
mint
pinch
pink
pond
print
punch
punk
quench
sent
tank
wench
went
wink

Unit 31

S	C	S	K	S	M

S	N	S	P	S	W

escape
scan
scar
scart
scat
skid
skin
skip
skunk
smack
smart
smash
smile
smock
smug
snack
snail
snake
snap
snarl
snatch
sneak
sniff

snip

snub

Spain

spam

spark

speak

speed

spend

spike

spin

spine

spit

spite

spook

spoon

spot

spun

swam

sweep

sweet

swim

swipe

Swiss

switch

swoon

Unit 32

~ N G

ban

bang

banging

Bangkok

Bangladesh

Beijing

bring

bringing

British

cling

drinking

doing

Dutch

eating

English

fling

French

going

Greek

hang

Hong Kong

king

long

playing

rang

reading

ring

ringing

rung

sang

saying

Shanghai

sing

singing

slang

sling

song

speaking

sting

stung

swing

Swiss

swung

wing

Unit 33

O R O R E A W

born

chore

core

dawn

door

draw

drawn

floor

for

fork

four

fourteen

jaw

law

lawn

moor

more

morning

or

poor

prawn

saw

score

short

sort

sport

store

storm

swore

torch

your

Unit 34

O W O U

about

brown

cloud

clown

count

cow

crowd

crown

down

drown

found

fountain

gown

ground

hound

how

loud

morning

mount

mountain

noun

now

out

Ow!

pound

proud

prow

round

shout

snout

sound

town

vow

Wow!

Unit 35

~	Y

angry
buy
by
byte
choppy
cloudy
cry
daddy
Danny
dry
fly
funny
Getty
grubby
guy
happy
hi-fi
hippy
hungry
jetty
lobby
lorry
may
megabyte
mummy
my
nanny
ply
pry
rainy
say
shy
silly
sky
slay
sly
spy
sunny
try
why
Wi-Fi
windy

Unit 36

O	Y	~	O	I	~

annoy
annoying
avoid
avoiding
boil
boiling
boy
coil
coin
coy
employ
enjoy
enjoying
foil
join
joining
joint
joy
loin
loyal
oil
point
pointing
royal
sol
soy
soya
spoil
toil
toy

Unit 37

I	R	U	R	O	R

bird
blur
burn
burning
burst
church
curl
first
flirt
fur
girl
Hamburg

her
herb
lurk
shirt
sir
skirt
spur
stir
surf
surfing
swirl
tore
turban
turf
Turk
turn
turning
whirl
word
wore
work
working
world
worm
worst

Unit 38

~	C	E	C	E	~	C	I	~

ace
cement
cent
centigrade
centigram
central
cert
certain
choice
cinema
circus
cite
citrus
civic
civil
cycling
dice
face
fake
fleece

force
ice
ice cream
Kent
kite
mice
Mike
nice
pace
peace
place
plaice
price
race
rake
rice
slice
space
spice
spike
trace
twice
vice
voice

Unit 39

| ~ | E | R |

banker
beefburger
better
bigger
boiler
border
browser
burger
butter
copper
farmer
fatter
hammer
hotter
letter
litter
manner
matter
order
pepper
pointer

power
printer
rubber
scanner
shower
singer
sleeper
sneaker
spammer
speaker
steamer
swimmer
tipper
toaster
trainer
waiter
winner
worker

Unit 40

| E | E | R | E | A | R | E | R | E |

beard
cheer
cheering
clear
dear
deer
ear
earring
fear
gear
hearing
here
jeer
near
peer
rear
sneer
spear
tear
we're
year

Unit 41

| A | I | R | ~ | A | R | E |

air
airfare

airport
armchair
bare
care
chair
dairy
dare
fair
fairy
fare
flare
glare
hair
hairy
hare
mare
pair
rare
scare
share
spare
square
stair
stairs

Unit 42

| E | W | U | E |

blew
blue
brew
chew
chewing
clue
crew
cue
dew
drew
due
few
fewer
flew
flue
glue
grew
new
newer
pew
queue

queuing
stew
stewing
sue
true

Unit 43

| ~ | E | L | L | | ~ | I | L | L |
| ~ | A | L | L | | ~ | U | L | L |

all
ball
bell
bill
bull
call
chill
cill
ell
fall
fell
fill
full
grill
hall
hill
ill
kill
mall
mill
pill
pull
quill
sell
shell
silly
skill
small
smell
spell
squall
stall
still
tall
tell
till
villa
wall

well
will

Unit 44

~	I	G	H	T
~	O	U	G	H	T
~	A	U	G	H	T
~	E	I	G	H	T

ate
bought
bright
brought
caught
eighteen
eighty
fight
flight
fought
fright
height
high
light
midnight
might
neighbour
night
nought
ought
right
sigh
sight
sign
slight
tight
weigh
weight

Unit 45

| U | ~ | E |

amuse
crude
cube
cute
dude
duke
dune

fluke
flute
fuse
June
Luke
lute
muse
music
prude
prune
reduce
rude
rule
ruler
tube
tune
use

Unit 46

| ~ | (| T | T |) | L | E |
| ~ | (| T |) | L | E |

able
apple
battle
Beatles
beetle
bible
bottle
bubble
cable
cattle
cradle
cripple
cuddle
dazzle
drizzle
fable
fiddle
gable
giggle
goggle
google
griddle
hobble
kettle
little
middle

muddle
needle
noodle
paddle
puddle
raffle
rifle
ripple
rubble
settle
shuttle
sizzle
table
tattle
title
wobble

Unit 47

`~` `O` `L` `D` `~` `O` `U` `L` `D`

boulder
cold
colder
could
fold
folder
folding
gold
hold
holding
mould
mouldy
old
older
should
shoulder
sold
told
would

Unit 48

`T` `H` `T` `H` `~` `~` `T` `H`

`~` `T` `H` `E`

birth
both
breath
breathe
further

gather
maths
mouth
north
soothe
south
teeth
than
thank
that
thaw
them
then
thick
thin
thing
third
thirsty
thirteen
thirty
this
thought
three
thrill
with
youth

Unit 49

`1` `2` `1` `S` `T` `2` `N` `D`

`3` `R` `D` `4` `T` `H`

bun
eighth
eighty
eleventh
fifth
fifty
first
forty
fourth
fun
gun
ninety
ninth
one
rum
second
seventh

seventy
sixth
sixty
son
sun
tenth
third
thirteenth
thirty
to
twelfth
twenty
two
won

Unit 50

`S` `T` `R` `S` `P` `R` `S` `C` `R`

astra
explain
express
extra
extreme
scrap
scrape
scream
screen
screw
screwdriver
script
scroll
scruffy
scrum
sprain
sprat
spray
spring
sprite
sprout
sprung
spry
straight
strain
strap
stray
stream
street
strife
strike

striker
string
strip
stripe
stroll
strong
struck
struggle
strum

Unit 51

| ~ | N | G | L | E | | ~ | N | D | L | E |
| ~ | M | B | L | E | | ~ | M | P | L | E |

amble
ample
angle
bangle
bumble
bundle
bungle
candle
crumble
crumple
dimple
example
fondle
grumble
handle
jingle
jungle
pimple
ramble
rumble
sample
scramble
simple
single
spindle
strangle
thimble
trample
tremble
triangle

Unit 52

| ~ | G | E | | G | E | ~ |

advantage
age
agency
agent
baggage
budge
cage
Egypt
gem
gene
general
gent
gentle
germ
German
Germany
gin
gym
gypsum
huge
image
page
passengers
rage
sage
stage
stooge
surgery
village
wage

Unit 53

| O | O | U | O | W |

blow
blown
close
Coca-Cola
crow
flow
flown
glow
grow
grown
low
Microsoft

o'clock
Oh!
OK
open
pillow
post
radio
show
slow
slower
snow
solo
throw
thrown
toe
video
willow
window
woe
yellow

Unit 54

| P | H | ~ | G | H |

alpha
alphabet
cough
enough
graph
laugh
nephew
phantom
pharmacy
Philip
phone
phono
photo
photocopy
phrase
physical
physics
rough
sphere
telephone
tough
typhoid

Unit 55

K N G N W R W H

gnash
gnat
gnaw
honour
hour
knack
knee
knew
knickers
knife
knight
knit
knock
knot
know
knuckle
who
whole
whom
whose
Wrangler
wrap
wreck
wren
wrench
wring
wrinkle
wrist
write
writer
writing
wrong
wrote

pyre
said
their
they
tread
want
was
were
what

Unit 56

E A A I E Y E I R

A R E E R E I R E

bread
byre
dead
drier
flyer
grey
head
liar